Covert Operations
of the
CIA &
Israel's Mossad

Inside the
Covert Operations
of the
CIA &
Israel's Mossad

Joel Bainerman

SPi.
BOOKS
A Division of Shapolsky Publishers

*Inside the Covert Operations of
the CIA & Israel's Mossad*

S.P.I. BOOKS
A division of Shapolsky Publishers, Inc.

ISBN 1-56171-350-3

For any additional information, contact:

S.P.I. BOOKS/Shapolsky Publishers, Inc.
136 West 22nd Street
New York, NY 10011
212/633-2022 / FAX 212/633-2123

Manufactured in Canada

10 9 8 7 6 5 4 3 2 1

Contents

The Dark Side Of The Israeli-American Relationship

Throughout the 1980's Israel aided America in her covert wars against Communism and helped then Vice-President George Bush and then Director of the CIA William Casey "conquer the world." It is a sphere of American-Israel relations that is rarely seen or discussed by the circle of "conventional wisdom" experts who dominate Middle East policy circles.

As an Israeli I find myself in a difficult position when I report on these activities. In Israel, all reports on Israel's involvement in weapons sales or training of foreign government troops or rebel forces are heavily censored, denied, or dismissed as "Leftist" or "anti-Israel." I am neither.

My problem is that I don't think that Israel derives that much benefit from being America's subcontractor for covert operations against Communism, nor from the relatively small amounts of money they earn from selling light weapons and ammunition in the process. Worse, every time one of these covert operations was exposed, it would be Israel who had to take the rap in the media. Despite the misconception many journalists on the Left have that it was Israel entangling America in foreign policy predicaments, such as the Iran-Contra affair, the exact opposite was the case. America was calling the shots and sending Israel into these regional wars to either shore-up the forces of the right-wing government involved, or arm and train an anti-communist rebel group.

Although it isn't clear what the Reagan administration offered Israel in return for Israel's military support in these covert wars, one thing is for sure: Bush and Casey turned Israel into an imperialist junkie.

The reason Casey was so fond of Israel was that Israel was willing and able to perform covert operations on his behalf. Israel would do what the Congress forbade the U.S. government to do. Intelligence agencies maintain assets, people they can call upon for information. These people are not on the payroll, nor are they agents, but they can supply vital services or information. Israel was (and still is) America's intelligence asset.

While it has often been argued by supporters of

Israel that Israel has a geo-strategic interest in containing Communism, I don't buy it. What difference does it make to the welfare of Israel if there are communist takeovers in countries as far away as Central and Latin America or South East Asia?

Israel's supporters will claim that Israel needs to sell arms to these regimes because it needs to keep its arms industry busy in order to offset the cost of military production for its own defence needs. Yet most of Israel's lucrative weapons sales come from high-tech items and the refurbishing of older-model airplanes. Most of this work comes from countries in the stable and developed world. Few Israelis have ever bothered to consider the harm that this policy of serving as America's strongman does. Indeed, since much of the Israeli Knesset has no idea as to where Israeli-sanctioned forces are working, it's no wonder that the subject has never been debated in the hall of parliament but is instead shrouded in the ever-so secret world of "national security". How many Israelis have ever even thought of this question:

Does Israel have to supply weapons to every corrupt and ruthless regime just because the CIA wants us to?

The problem for Israel's image begins when it, as well as America, becomes associated with the hated regime as peasants get massacred by soldiers outfitted with Uzis and Galils.

Another problem with Israel arming foreign countries is the secrecy in which these deals must be shrouded. For instance, in May 1994 Deputy-Foreign Minister Yossi Beilin addressed the Knesset's Foreign Affairs committee and revealed that Israel had received a request from two countries to "help them deal with their internal conflicts," i.e., train their government troops or help keep the Communist rebels at bay. Knesset Member Gonen Segev demanded that Beilin reveal the name of the two countries but he refused, citing "national security." (*Yediot Aharonot*, May 19th, 1994)

Don't Israeli citizens have the right to know what countries their nation is supporting, covertly or overtly? What are the implications for Israel's democratic character when foreign policy is taken underground and conducted in total secrecy?

U.S.-Israeli Destabilization Efforts

It's not known who in the Reagan White House actually came up with the term "low intensity warfare" to describe the operation whereby proxy rebel armies would be used to destabilize un-cooperative Third World countries. However, a main player in this policy initiative was an overt institution called, The National Endowment for Democracy (NED), which the White House created in 1983. The charter of the NED was to "strengthen democratic institutions throughout the world through private, non-governmental efforts." Congress agreed to fund NED only after CIA Director William Casey assured it that the CIA would not utilize NED for covert activities. Casey lied.

The following is but a partial list of some of the causes supported by NED, with Israel's help:

Seychelles: On November 29th,1981, *The Sunday Tribune* of Durban, South Africa, reported that the CIA was behind a failed mercenary invasion of the island nation. An armed battle at the Seychelles National Airport was about as far as the rebellion got.

Surinam: On July 18th, 1983, the *Reuters* news service reported that a planned invasion of Surinam was being carried out with the help of Florida-based mercenaries. However it was later called off when the Netherlands internal security agencies uncovered it. The Dutch News Agency reported on July 1st that 300 mercenaries left from the coast of Florida for Paramaribo, in the former Dutch colony. Half of the mercenaries were from the United States. The objective of the mission was to oust Surinam strongman Lt. Colonel Dasibouterse. The news agency said mercenaries would have been supported later by exiled Surinames recruited in The Netherlands, who would have entered Surinam from neighboring French Guyana.

Libya: In a report in 1987 in the *Washington Post*, Bob Woodward revealed that Robert Gates, while deputy director of the CIA, had presented a plan to the White House that would "re-draw the map of North Africa." It was accepted by the White House, but later rejected by the State Department. Part of that scenario included capturing half of Libya's territories. (*In These Times*, February 15th, 1989)

With the aim of overthrowing Libyan strongman Muammar Khadafy, Israel and the U.S. trained anti-Libyan rebels in a number of West and Central African countries. The Paris-based *African Confidential* newsletter reported on January 5th, 1989, that the U.S. and Israel had set up a series of bases in Chad and other neighboring countries to train 2000 Libyan rebels captured by the Chad army.

The group, called The National Front for the Salvation of Libya, was based in Chad. Israel trained at least 30 Libyan pilots at Ndele in the northern part of the Central African Republic, a service which probably had something to do with that country's recognition of Israel in February 1989. Israel also provided training facilities for the Libyan rebels in Cameroon at Kaele and Djoum, with the CIA providing the weapons.

A recruiting office was opened in Zaire's capital of Kinshasa and 50 anti-Khadafy Libyans were being trained by Gabonese head of state Omar Bongo's presidential-guard in Wonga Wonga as well as at Ndele, an Israeli base in the Central African Republic.

Chad: The CIA provided arms and money to Hissene Habrew in his attempt to overthrow the government of Goukouni Oueddei. The operation was coordinated with Egypt, and according to Jay Peterzell in his book, *Reagan's Secret Wars* (National Security Studies 1984), Sudan provided both a base for operations and a supply line. In June 1982 Habrew took control of the capital of Chad and established a provisional government.

Mozambique: According to a series of press reports, the most detailed one appearing in the London-based *Independent* newspaper of November 30th, 1986, Israel helped anti-government rebels in Mozambique overthrow the government. Israeli military advisers were also believed to be operating in Malawi, which was used as a base by the National Resistance Movement guerrillas in the Tete province of Mozambique near the Malawi border.

A report in *African Analysis* claimed this guerrilla movement received extensive Israeli military instruction. Paulo Oliveria, a Lisbon-based spokesperson, told journalists in Maputo in 1988 that National Resistance Members received training from Israeli military. The March 24th, 1988 *Guardian* newspaper in London quoted Oliviera as saying that "hundreds of these rebels were sent to Israel for extensive training."

A former South African Military intelligence official, Roland Hunter, told the publication *South Scan* in April 1991 that during the early 1980s Israel was the channel for Eastern European weapons supplied by South Africa to anti-Mozambique rebels. These included AK-47 rifles and RPGs made in Romania, Bulgaria, and Czechoslovakia.

Angola: The 1976 Clark Amendment prohibited U.S. assistance to the National Union for the Total Independence of Angola (UNITA), the South African-based army fighting the Marxist Angolan government since the country gained its independence from Portugal in 1975. Sam Bamieh, a U.S. businessman of Arab decent, told Congressional investigating committees that he was asked by the Saudi government in 1983 to help channel more than $50 million to UNITA as part of the AWACS deal. He claimed William Casey personally solicited the aid. In May 1986, *African Report* noted that since 1982 the U.S. government had supplied UNITA with weapons through intermediaries in

Saudi Arabia, Israel and Zaire. (*In These Times*, Oct 28th, 1987)

After the Clark Amendment ban was lifted in 1985, more than $13 million were given to Joans Savimbi's UNITA forces. By 1988 the CIA was spending more than $45 million annually to back Savimbi.

In 1990, the Angolan government accused the U.S., Israel and Zaire of planning to topple its regime. The idea for this mission, code-named COMA, is attributed to retired Israeli colonel Meir Meytuas, who at the time was employed by the Republic of Cameroon as a security adviser to President Paul Biya. Documents released to the publication *Southscan* in June, 1990 by Andre Panzo, Angola's charge d'affaires in Zimbabwe, showed Meytuas to be a close friend of Zaire's President Mobutu.

The Norbistor Affair

No better example of a joint Israel-America covert operation to bring down a foreign government can be found than the Norbistor Affair. Unfortunately for the White House, it didn't go quite as planned.

Sometime in late 1984 the two governments planned a coup to overthrow Jerry Rawlings,

President of the West African republic of Ghana.

Why would the U.S. want to overthrow Ghana?

Relations between the Reagan administration and the left-leaning government of Jerry Rawlings were never very friendly, particularly since Rawlings had good relations with Libya's Muammar Khadafy.

In July 1985 a relative of Rawlings became romantically involved with Sharon Scrannage, a young woman who worked for the CIA. She allegedly turned over the names and information about CIA agents who had penetrated the Ghanaian government. After the mercenaries were captured and awaiting trial in Brazil, one of them wrote from his prison cell:

"Jerry Rawlings has pissed off not only the Company (the CIA) but its cousin (the Mossad) in the Middle East."

By involving itself in this covert operation Israel was hoping to spring one of its agents, held by Ghana after he was exposed as a CIA employee.

The coup was a joint venture of Solomon Schwartz, a low-level intelligence operative of both the CIA and Mossad, as the key contact between Argentina, the Israelis, the South Africans, and the State Department's Office of West African Affairs.

Schwartz had good contacts in Argentina. Through Kevin Kattke, a rogue agent who worked for Oliver North in the Caribbean, he was introduced to Godfrey Osei. Osei told one of the mercenaries involved in the plot: "I came to Washington with no experience and I went to the front door of the CIA. They put me on hold for a couple of years. Then, things started happening."

The CIA put people in contact with him and in early 1986 everything started to come together. No one quite knew who Osei was. He had been imprisoned on fraud charges in Ghana, and presented himself to the mercenaries as a former Defence Minister in Rawlings' government. He told the Argentine authorities he was an envoy of the Ghanian Defence Ministry and was authorized to purchase $200,000 worth of weapons, munitions and explosives from the Argentine army production conglomerate, Fabricaciones Militares.

To procure financing for the operation, Osei offered a seaside gambling concession to the Chinese Mafia in New York, who backed the coup with $500,000. He also promised one of the mercenaries, Ted Bishop, cocoa and coffee marketing rights in Ghana.

It was Bishop who arranged the purchase of 6 tons of weapons for the job. According to mercenary Timothy Carmody, Bishop was the connection to Schwartz, who, he was told, was an agent for Israeli intelligence and worked out of the offices of Botswana International in New York. In

November 1986 investigative journalist Jack Anderson contacted Solomon Schwartz at a company called B International in New York.

Bishop told the mercenaries that the plot was sanctioned by the White House. He would often boast to them that he had "walk-in access to the highest office in the land- the National Security Council." (*San Francisco Chronicle*, November 11th, 1986) and that he worked for a "lieutenant colonel" who worked for "an admiral" at the National Security Council (NSC). When they were eventually caught, one of the mercenaries repeated what Bishop had told him, "I worked for the National Security Council and I report to a Marine colonel in Room 357 of the White House Executive Office Building."

John Early of Albuquerque, was the military leader of the mercenaries. He was a contributing editor to *Soldier of Fortune* magazine, operated a parachute training school in Albuquerque, and spent nearly four years in the Rhodesian air force. Those who knew him said he was a "shadowy figure" involved in clandestine activities both in Laos in the 1960's and later in El Salvador.

The mission task-force consisted of one Argentine and eight American Vietnam veterans. Their six week mission was to escort the six tons of weapons and rendezvous with a ship off the Ghana coast. The weapons were purchased from the Argentine army, which also transported and loaded them on the vessel. An attack on the city of Accra would follow. They would then train a force of 100 Ghanaian dissidents to overthrow Rawlings. The plan also included the freeing of CIA agents imprisoned by Rawlings and destroying a Libyan training center.

The plot was doomed from the start. The equipment and arms were less than adequate. The boat to transport them to Africa arrived two weeks late. Then, the Argentine captain wanted another $50,000 for the trip.

Early began to get suspicious about Bishop when he failed to show up for the final certification of the cargo by port authorities. After he had a Tampa private detective check Osei out he discovered that Osei had no official ties whatsoever to the Ghana government. The mercenaries began to question their mission and the person in charge, Solomon Schwartz. Six hundred miles off the Brazilian coast they decided their mission was compromised and that they might get killed in Africa.

When they turned back and ran ashore north of Rio De Janeiro the Brazilian police suspected they were going to sell the weapons they had onboard to right-wing landowners in order to resist a proposed land reform. The police seized the boat and its cargo and put the men in jail.

Early and the Argentine captain were sentenced to five years in prison and the other seven Americans to four years. When Carmody told his wife he needed "iron enriched" tablets she knew exactly what he meant and sent him four hacksaw blades in a box of powdered milk. (*The Atlanta Journal*, December 27th, 1986)

On December 15th, 1986, he and three others escaped by climbing down the prison walls with a ladder made out of knotted sheets. With the help of bush pilots who took them the distance in several short hops they made it through the jungle to La Paz, Bolivia. In late February 1987 the remaining mercenaries were extradited to Argentina, where they jumped bail and returned to the U.S.

The CIA and Solomon Schwartz have denied any involvement in the operation. The State Department said the men were operating as free agents, yet throughout the affair Schwartz's telephone records showed that he was in continuous contact with the State Department's West Africa desk. Two U.S. government officials claim that Godfrey Osei kept in close contact with the State Department's Office of West African Affairs about his coup plans. Ed Perkins, then head of that office and later Ambassador to South Africa, acknowledged to Foster that he had met with

Osei in late 1985 but insisted that the "routine meeting" was held at Osei's request. He denied knowing Osei very well or supporting his plans.

Another official from the NSC who moved over to the CIA in 1987, says that sometime in late 1985 Ambassador Perkis referred Ghanian rebels seeking U.S. help in a coup attempt to the NSC. The official claims that the meeting was held in an attempt to "discourage, rather than promote", the effort to overthrow Rawlings.

It is extremely difficult to believe that Solomon Schwartz would contract this job out to a group of private mercenaries if he wasn't acting on behalf of the U.S. government. How many individuals acting on their own decide to stage a coup?

Post Cold War American-Israel Covert Operations

Is this stuff still going on? You bet.

For instance, throughout 1992 Israel forged impressive but confusing ties throughout the former Soviet bloc. One example is the suddenly warm friendship between Israel and Kazakhstan, a predominantly Shiite Central Asian republic. (*Inside Israel*, March 1993)

In early fall 1992, Richard Armitage of the U.S. Agency for International Development (AID) signed an agreement with Ehud Gol, director of the Israeli Foreign Ministry's Division for International Cooperation (Mashav), that committed both nations to improving the economic infrastructure of Kazakhstan.

On the surface the agreement appeared modest in scope; the financial commitment was only $4 million. A subsequent visit to Washington by Economics Minister Shimon Shetreet led to the release of far more daunting statistics. The $4 million was a tiny downpayment on a program that totalled $400 million for one year in direct assistance. Where the money was earmarked for was never made public.

Of great interest is the work portfolio of Richard Armitage. After serving in Theodore Shackley's Saigon CIA station until the city's fall, he was reassigned to Bangkok where he was employed by the State Department as a consultant on refugee affairs. In 1987, Ross Perot accused Armitage of running a CIA station in Bangkok which profited from drug connections. Armitage's office was suspected of being a money conduit to Teheran and the Australian bank Nugan Hand, which later became entangled in a huge embezzlement scandal implicating former and current CIA agents.

Armitage's co-signatory, Mashav, recruits students from the Third World for technical courses in Israel and sends Israeli technicians and scientists to the Third World to set up, for the most part, agricultural and health related projects. But as Mashav sometimes boasts, there are other dividends. For instance, thanks to contacts made in the farming sector, the Philippines were persuaded to buy Israeli armaments, including 18 Kfir fighter jets.

Meanwhile, The Dutch press service IPS reported in early 1993 that the Shiite republic of Azerbaijan, locked in a bloody war with Armenia over disputed territory, had been the recipient of Israeli arms including Stinger missiles and communications equipment. Israel and the U.S. seemed to be playing a background role in other areas of the former Soviet Union. When Radio Abkhazia reported in May 1993 that Iran-Contra player and Israeli arms merchant Yaakov Nimrodi had sold a planeload of weapons to Georgia, the item caused furious denials by Georgian Prime Minister Tangiz Seegoa and President Edward Shevardnadze. (*Inside Israel*, June 1993)

Abkhazia was at the time fighting a war of secession with Georgia and receiving military aid from Russia. Shevardnadze has admitted that Nimrodi did offer an arms deal but claims he turned it down. The final arrangement was that Georgia would trade mineral water for Israeli chickens, mutton and rice. Since Georgia has no shortage of sheep and Israel does not grow rice, the journalists he was addressing were naturally skeptical.

Shevardnadze challenged them to visit the ship when it docked to witness the rice being unloaded. He concluded his meeting with the ambiguous statement, "Even if it was true that we cut an arms deal with Nimrodi, is that any worse than the Russians supplying Abkhazia?"

According to a high-ranking Georgian official, Nimrodi was accompanied to his meeting with Shevardnadze by a KGB agent named Vasilav, who purported to be the Head of the Russian Academy of Science. Vasilav has a great deal in common with Eliah Zemtsov, a Soviet scientist who arrived in Israel in 1971 and was put to work by the Likud a decade later to arrange a Shamir/Gorbachev summit. According to Israeli President, Ezer Weizman, Zemtsov has,"one foot in the CIA and one in the KGB."

At the time of Nimrodi's visit Zemtsov was ensconced in the guest house of the Georgian government for reasons as yet undisclosed. Nimrodi's calm response to the allegations was, "The reporters are a bunch of liars. Who are you going to believe, them or Shevardnaze?"

This little obfuscation did little to sidetrack *Abkazia Radio*, which continued to insist that Georgia was receiving arms from Israel via Nimrodi, denials or no denials.

Another area where Israel played an active role is in Serbia.

According to a March 1993 report in *The European* newspaper, the Mossad, in cooperation with an American Jewish organization believed to be the Joint Distribution Committee (JDC), is "rescuing" Serbian Jews by land and sea as part of a secret deal with Serbia exchanging them for Israeli weapons. The report said that the Mossad has carried out three missions bringing out 500 Jews.

The newspaper quotes European diplomats as saying there are "rumors everywhere that Israelis are violating the international embargo, although nothing has been proven."

The Ministry of Defence denied the charge claiming that "Israel is following the embargo 100%." Israeli officials have dismissed the story, noting that Serbian Jews are in no danger and are free to emigrate. One major player alleged to be involved in covert Israel-Serbian arms sales is a new Israeli immigrant, Jezdimir Vasileivitch. (*Inside Israel*, September 1993)

In July 1993, Vasileivitch, owner of the Yugoskondik Bank, Serbia's largest, arrived in Israel to donate 50,000 Swiss Francs to a Zionist youth village. Rumors that he had transferred $2 billion out of the country initiated a run on his bank and within a week of his arrival he announced that he would not be returning home but rather applying to the Interior Ministry for permanent residency. The Interior Ministry denied his request and his current whereabouts are unknown.

Vasileivitch, who is not Jewish, made much of his money in two particular ways; he and an Israeli partner violated the UN embargo on Iraqi oil, and he exploited the international currency markets with Serbia's inflated money. Eastern European diplomatic sources claim that Serbian President Slobodan Milosevich permitted Vasileivitch to transfer over a billion dollars of the country's foreign reserves to Bank Leumi where at least part of the money was used to fund arms deals. Vasileivitch admits to having business interests in Israel but insists that they are confined to paper products and pharmaceuticals, not weapons.

One American reporter who arrived in Israel from Eastern Europe claims that after Vasileivitch absconded with a good chunk of his country's public savings, "a number of contracts were put out on him."

Israel is also active in Africa, probably at American instigation. In late December 1992, soldiers rioted in Zaire killing about 300 people including the French Ambassador Phillip Bernard. The soldiers had just received their paychecks in new currency issued by President Sesa Seko Mobuto when Prime Minister Etian Cheskadi declared the money invalid.

Mobuto quelled the riot with his elite forces, the DSP, which were trained by Israelis. According to Zaire radio, Israel's military attache to Zaire visited DSP headquarters the day the riots erupted to offer advice. Once the uprising was under control the DSP began a manhunt which brutally eliminated over a hundred of the protesters.

Since its deep involvement in Angola, along with the U.S., in the late 1980s, Israel's relations with Angloa have traditionally been very cool. However, Angolan President Jose Eduardo dos Santos had a remarkable change of heart. Until September 1993, Israel supported dos Santo's bitter rival Jonas Savimbi of the American-backed rebels UNITA. Then dos Santos defeated

Savimbi in a legitimate election and both Israel and America decided to support the new government. (*Inside Israel*, May 1993)

Naturally, the Israeli support involved covert military assistance. An alleged former Mossad agent known as "Colonel Yossi" is the commander of hundreds of Israeli and South African mercenaries protecting the current regime against UNITA forces. The South Africans are guarding American companies' oil installations while the Israelis are engaged in actual combat.

The mercenaries are paid well for the risks they take. Foot soldiers receive $2500 a month to start while officers collect well over $10,000.

Colonel Yossi claims he is the head of a security company called 'Ango-Sago' hired to protect only U.S. oil facilities. However, his small army of Israelis is fighting far from any oil depots.

Israel's about-face coincides with a similar White House change of policy towards Savimbi. America seems to feel its oil and other economic interests are better served by dos Santos with the protection of Israelis.

In February 1994 Israeli TV revealed that a large delegation of Israeli reserve officers, led by General Zev Zakhran, were in the Congo and training government forces. (*Inside Israel*, March 1994)

They brought with them a significant armory worth millions of dollars, including small arms, rockets, and helicopters. The goal of the officers is to put down an insurrection by the Liberal Party of the Congo. The opposition movement has the support of 70% of the country's population and is in effective control of much of the hinterland.

The rebels, clearly frightened of the Israelis, sent a fax to an unnamed Israeli colonel, offering $12 million upfront as well as the rights to exploit the country's vast resources of oil, gold, diamonds, uranium and timber. In return, the colonel was asked to supply the soldiers and weapons needed to overthrow the current regime.

This is not the first time that an Israeli Minister has taken an undue interest in this little African country. Three weeks before the first democratic elections in the Congo in 1992, three Israeli "radio technicians" landed in the capital of Brazaville along with their two French employers. Two weeks later they were arrested leaving the country and accused of attempting to foment unrest. (*Inside Israel,* November 1992)

The three Israelis were captured with army communications equipment. They were employed by a company called Shaphron, which is headed by three former military intelligence officials, one of whom, Rafi Khazak, was in line to head the Shabak (General Security Services), Israel's internal security service, when he became embroiled in a personal scandal.

Only the personal intervention of Foreign Minister Shimon Peres, who prevailed on the French and American governments to intervene, secured the release of the three.

In yet another part of Africa, it appears that Israel is playing a role in arming Sudanese Christian rebels, most likely on America's behalf.

In late March 1994, a Nigerian Boeing 707 flew out of Ben Gurion Airport on its way to Cairo for "refuelling." The Egyptians turned the plane away and it landed at Nicosia Airport in Cyprus. There it developed engine trouble and had to delay departure just long enough to raise the suspicions of the Cypriot authorities who ordered that the plane be searched. What was discovered was a huge airborne armory. (*Inside Israel*, April 1994)

The Nigerian crew claimed that the arms were destined for Uganda, a charge vigorously denied by both the Israeli Foreign Ministry, which insisted it had no knowledge whatsoever of the flight's cargo, and the Ugandan government. According to one Ugandan official quoted in the government newspaper *New Vision Daily*, "Uganda has no diplomatic, economic or military ties to Israel and there is no reason to suspect us in this matter."

So what was the destination of the shipment? According to Sudanese President, General Omar El Bashir, the arms were on their way to Sudanese Christian rebels based in the south of the country who were waging a defensive war against his Islamic fundamentalist regime.

Press reports more than suggest that the U.S., Britain, Egypt and Saudi Arabia have given the green light to arming the rebels with Israeli weapons. In fact, the arms were finally loaded onto a British plane whence, presumably, they continued on their originally planned itinerary.

The one hitch is Egyptian involvement. Why would a 707 need to refuel in Cairo when its range would easily take it from Israel to southern Sudan? Clearly, the intended landing had another purpose.

And if Egypt was involved in the operation to support Sudanese rebels, why did it refuse landing rights to the Nigerian plane?

The Strange Saga of
Ari Ben Menashe

If they gave out a "Man of the Year" award to the
most controversial covert operator the 1991 prize
would go to Ari Ben Menashe. He was, for me, a
window onto the American-Israeli secret world.

Until the summer of 1991 nobody had heard
about Ari Ben Menashe. Yet in a very short period
of time he became Israel's most famous informant
as articles about him appeared in *Time* and
Newsweek. His claim that press baron Robert Maxwell was involved in arms sales to Iran, closely
followed by Maxwell's mysterious death, rocketed
him to international notoriety and recognition.

Who was this Israeli intelligence agent spinning intriguing tales about American and Israeli
covert operations? And what were his motives?

Martin Kilian of *Der Spiegel* told me that Ben
Menashe had a copy of Amiram Nir's diaries. At
that time Nir's mysterious death in Mexico was

the key focus of my research.

From April-May 1991 I spent a good deal of time with Ben Menashe. We met in Cincinnati airport then at Los Angeles and spoke on the phone several times. At our first meeting we spent the entire morning and a good part of the afternoon weaving in and out of ten years of secret agendas in the Reagan and Bush White Houses. Among them: how the current director of the CIA Robert Gates had helped Iraq gain chemical weapons capabilities; the "October Surprise" allegations that the Reagan campaign team deliberately delayed the release of the 52 American hostages held in Iran in order to influence the Presidential election of 1980; the Inslaw case, a Washington, D.C. computer company which had its prize software stolen by a crony of former Attorney General Edwin Meese.

Ben Menashe asserted that Israeli and American arms sales to Iran and Iraq were in fact far more extensive than was publicly known, and that the Israeli government had earned $800 million in commission on more than $80 billion of arms sold to Iran throughout the eight-year war. The money, he said, had accumulated in slush funds secreted in several Latin American banks. Probably the most outlandish claim of all was that former director of the National Security Council Robert McFarlane was an "Israeli agent."

I walked away with my head spinning.

In April 1989 Ben Menashe was caught in a U.S. Customs sting operation and charged with conspiring to violate the Arms Export Control Act. He was trying to sell three Israeli-owned C-130 Hercules transport airplanes to Iran without the State Department approval needed for resale of U.S. made military goods. After a six week trial in November 1990, however, he was acquitted.

Ben Menashe asserts that from 1987-1989 he was a member of the elite Israeli intelligence unit that was run directly out of Prime Minister Yitzhak Shamir's office. The sale of the three C-130s, Ben Menashe asserts, was part of an arms-for-hostages deal for the release of three Israeli soldiers held in Lebanon.

He also claims to have worked on a special team, called The Joint Israeli Defence Force Military Intelligence/Mossad Committee for Iran-Israel Relations, set up in November 1980 as part of the "October Surprise" deal, to supply American-made arms through Israel to Iran. The operation was run jointly by the Mossad and Israeli military intelligence. (*Esquire*, October 1991)

When he was first arrested, the Israeli government denied any knowledge of him. Then, it was claimed that he was nothing more than a lowly translator, "All the work he did for us was done in his room while sitting at his word processor," claimed Ben Menashe's last boss, a colonel in Israeli military intelligence, (*Time* July 1st, 1991)

In August 1983 the colonel wanted to send him to the Israeli military attache's office in Washington to work as a translator. After he appeared before a committee for a routine job qualification examination, their conclusion was: "The man suffers from serious mental disorders." Why didn't the military intelligence service not then throw this man who suffered from "serious mental disorders" out of the service?

During his trial, the Israeli government spokesman in New York Yuval Rotem told reporters that Ben Menashe was "known to the defence establishment as an impostor who introduced himself several times with different identification in various countries as though serving in a high ranking position." The Israeli government also submitted an affidavit to the court stating that neither Shamir nor Pazner had ever heard of Ben-Menashe.

The question, however, isn't what position Ben Menashe held, but rather, the quality of his information. Too many people hastily dismissed him as a charlatan. What they didn't realize was that he was surfacing from another world. A world most people don't even know exists, let alone ever come into contract with.

Although Ben Menashe claims he participated

in many of the scandals he was exposing, I don't believe he did. Nor does it really matter if he did or didn't, or whether he learned about them from first or second hand sources. What remains pertinent are the events he describes. He's simply a mouthpiece, a window into a covert world. It is up to investigative journalists and Congressional committees to verify his allegations.

The July 1st, 1991 piece in *Time* was the first major story on Ben Menashe. Yet instead of giving him the benefit of the doubt and going out to investigate his claims, the reporter summarily concluded he was a charlatan. Thus anything he said was not credible but mere "conspiracy theories."

The rest of the mainstream press were convinced that since Ben Menashe was lying, there was no "October Surprise" and the only arms the U.S. had sold to Iran had come under the $50 million that Reagan claimed would "fit in one cargo plane."

It was all or nothing. Either Ben Menashe was 100% accurate, or the official story of Iran Contra was correct. Since Ben Menashe lied about a few details, the Reagan administration was not involved in any of the alleged secret agendas and covert operations. Every investigative journalist with information about members of the Administration's dirty deeds must have, therefore, also been, like Ben Menashe, out merely to smear the White House.

Hirsh Goodman, editor-in-chief of *The Jerusalem Report*, is a good example of the ignorance of the mainstream press. The *Report* came out in the fall of 1990 as a weekly news magazine on Middle East and Israeli affairs. It was well financed by the Bronfman family, owners of the Seagrams whisky fortune, and competed directly with *The Jerusalem Post* to be the primary source of English-language news from Israel. It was only after I had begun working for it that I realized that rather than being an independent publication seeking to provide in-depth reporting on what is really happening in Israel (i.e., the truth), it was mostly a mouthpiece for Bronfman and/or the Israeli government.

After meeting Ben Menashe in April 1991 I returned to Israel and began working as a freelance journalist for *The Report*. In late July, Amiram Nir's house in Tel Aviv had been broken into and tape recordings he had made of Israeli and American arms sales to Iran were stolen. By this time I had already been researching Nir's role in Irangate for nearly two years. I wanted to write a major piece for *The Jerusalem Report* on him. Here was my lead.

When I brought the story to one of the senior editors he suggested I contact Nir's sister, who worked for a local cable TV company. I wrote her a short letter asking for an interview. About a week later, Goodman called me into his office and asked me to explain why I had written this letter. When I did so, he went ballistic and he told me I would never be able to write for his publication again and that if I set foot inside the building he would have me arrested. When I asked him to explain why he was so angry, he mumbled something about "integrity in journalism" and then threatened to sue me. For what, he never said.

Only a few days later did I realize what had happened. A couple of weeks before the Nir break-in I gave managing editor Zev Chefets a piece I wrote about Ben Menashe and his claims. He said he knew little of Iran Contra but would pass it on to Goodman, who followed the subject as a defence reporter for *The Jerusalem Post*. Hirsh refused to use the story, claiming that he knew Ben Menashe to be a liar and not credible. He had never met the man, yet he knew he was a liar.

Here was the complete prejudice of the mainstream press at work.

Despite Goodman's apparent expertise and extensive knowledge of the inner workings of the Israeli defence establishment, he actually believed Israel and America's official story that Iran Contra was about trading $50 million worth arms to release a few hostages. Known for his inflated ego,

Goodman was either too jealous that someone could come along and dare to know more about a subject he was supposed to be an expert on, or, as others have suggested, the magazine was serving as a mouthpiece for certain elements in the Israeli and Jewish establishments which didn't want to see any of the truth about these covert operations exposed. Had I the resources of *The Report* at my disposal, we could have had an ongoing investigation and made a real contribution to uncovering the truth. Instead, Goodman believed Israeli government officials when they told him that Ben Menashe was a phony.

Goodman is an example of all that is wrong in the press today. Instead of investigating reports on his own to seek out the truth, he was prepared to print what some spokesperson in a government ministry told him to. Few reporters and editors who "knew Ben Menashe was lying" bothered to take the time to read the transcripts of his trial. They reveal that, at the very least, Ben Menashe had access to information on Irangate at least two months before the scandal broke.

His attorney Thomas Dunn subpoenaed Raji Samghabadi, a former *Time* reporter who was one of the first journalists to break the story of major arms sales to Iran in July 1983. In September 1986 at the Algonquin Hotel in New York City, Ben Menashe, by his account on the order of Shamir, gave Samghabadi details about former National Security Adviser Robert McFarlane's secret trip to Teheran in May 1986. Shamir wanted the story to appear and embarrass his rival, Labor party leader Shimon Peres. Samghabadi's editors refused to publish the account because they couldn't get confirmation from other sources.

Dunn told the court that subsequently Ben Menashe started demanding a higher position within the secret services. Pressure was put on Shamir to get rid of him as he was getting "too big for his britches."

"Ari was fired in September 1987," Dunn told the court. "But Shamir really liked him because Ari is his boy and Ari does his deals. He tells him, Ari, you are out, but you are not out. You are going to report directly to me."

Dunn claimed that the reason Ben Menashe was set-up to get stung by U.S. Customs was his refusal to turn over the $600 million plus $2 million in interest earned from commissions on Israeli arms sales to Iran to Prime Minister Shamir. Ben Menashe was supposedly part of a small group of people who had access to money stowed away in a consortium of South American banks. Ben Menashe claimed that besides himself two other people controlled the accounts, individually and collectively, and that all three were tied to the Israeli government.

"Other commissions on arms sales to Iran went to build settlements in the territories, and were funneled through the agricultural and housing ministries," Ben Menashe says. "It enabled the Likud party to fund part of its election campaign."

Ben Menashe said he wanted to expose these and other scandals because he was angry at Israel for not coming to his aid during his trial and for letting him sit in jail for over a year.

"They thought I was going to be a good boy and keep my mouth shut," he told me. "They were wrong. Not me."

Was he working with the Israeli government? It's difficult to believe he would have had access to the three C-130 planes had he not been affiliated in some manner with Israel. If he didn't believe the the planes were available for sale, why would he have met with potential buyers? Wherever the planes were stored, he had to have had official permission to move them if he arranged a sale. And it need not necessarily have been a government official, only someone he knew, who said to him, "find a buyer and you'll take your cut." He could also have approached an Israeli defense official and told him he had an Iranian customer for the aircraft.

In any event, the proof is in the pudding. The jury acquitted him. At least, they believed he was working for the Israeli government.

Some people believe Ben Menashe is simply an angry stool-pigeon. After being imprisoned he was embittered and looking for revenge. He was sitting in jail asking himself "why aren't they putting up my bail? Why aren't they paying my lawyer's bills? Those bastards, I'm going to screw them. When I get out of here they are going to be sorry."

Some people, however, don't buy that version either, insisting instead that Ben Menashe was still employed by the Israelis. For a while I too fell into that category. If Ben Menashe was really "out on his own" and was saying things which would embarrass Israel, he would be looking over his shoulder and in his shadow for Mossad. Yet never once during our interviews did he appear frightened. Nor did he appear so to other journalists. When I called him up and asked to meet with him he didn't know me from Adam. He didn't bother checking with anyone about who I was, just said: "Sure, let's meet."

I was convinced that Ben Menashe was working for Israel. Nearly all of his allegations were against the Reagan and Bush Administrations, not Israel. It seemed odd to me that for a guy who was supposed to be mad as hell at Israel, he wasn't too interested in dragging Israel's name through the mud.

I thought there was a covert operation going

on whereby Ben Menashe was serving as a mouthpiece for Shamir, telling the world everything Shamir wanted known. The underlying purpose was to keep Bush off-guard, to embarrass him and the previous Republican administration and to keep him at bay so he would stop pressuring Israel to leave the West Bank. When *New York Times* columnist Leslie Gelb described the so-called theft and airing of Amiram Nir's personal tape recordings on ABC's *News Nightline* in September 1991 as "an arrow shot across Bush's sails," I was convinced that I was right.

Then in the fall of 1991, Ben Menashe started to expose Israeli- related operations, such as Israel's nuclear arms program and how

Israel had traded information received from Jonathan Pollard to the Soviets. This shot down my theory. If he was working for Israel, would Shamir want that to be made known? The only answer I could come up with was that Shamir may be trying to "stick it to Bush," as if to say to him: "we did it, you know about it, and now everyone else knows it too." In other words, one gigantic mind game between Shamir and Bush. Two covert operators going head-to-head.

Regardless of whether he is still working for Israel or not, and regardless of any other ulterior motives he may have, what's important is Ben Menashe's information, not how he secured it. To determine the quality of that information means taking it out of his mouth and putting it into sequence and the context which surrounded the events.

CLAIM: Ben Menashe talked about The Joint Committee, also known as the Joint Israeli Defense Force Military Intelligence/Mossad Committee for Israel-Israel Relations, which was run by the Mossad and Israeli military intelligence. "We had tens and tens of companies that were opened and closed, middlemen and cover companies all over the world for these deals," he say. "But all of them were linked to the Joint Committee." (*Esquire*, October 1991)

FACT: On 25th September 1985, *Intelligence Digest*, a newsletter of the intelligence community, reported that "intelligence exchanges were made between Mossad and IRI Savama (Khomeini's secret service). Teams from Israel Aircraft Industries (IAI) were sent to Iran to overhaul Iranian air force jet engines. The Mossad established networks to coordinate weapons and spare parts procurement (to Iran) in Belgium, Britain, France, Greece, Cyprus, Denmark, and the United States. The vast global network, involving up to 2,000 people of numerous nationalities, soon expanded to Canada and West Germany."

That description sounds pretty close to what

The Joint Committee was and the activities in which it engaged.

Reports of U.S. and Israeli arms sales to Iran are too numerous to list. A more fundamental question is how much weaponry does it take to keep a war going for eight years? Could $82 billion, $10 billion a year, be an unreasonable figure for Iran to have spent on the war?

It doesn't matter what Ben Menashe claims about being part of that body. What seems incontestable is the existence of the Joint Committee.

CLAIM: Jonathan Pollard stole satellite pictures and data which were used to aim nuclear missiles at the Soviet Union. Some of this information was relayed by Prime Minister Yitzhak Shamir to the Soviets. The information was passed on to Yevgeny M. Primakov, the Soviet Foreign Ministry's specialist on the Middle East. (*Time*, October 28th, 1991)

In his book *The Samson Option*, Seymour Hersh, who used Ben Menashe as a primary source on the story, writes that Israel wanted Pollard to steal satellite pictures so that it could aim its missiles at targets inside the Soviet Union. To do this American intelligence information was needed about how the U.S. planned to achieve this goal. Another of Shamir's objectives was "to end the long-standing enmity between Israel and the Soviet Union and initiate some kind of strategic co-operation."

FACT: Hersh was not the first journalist to claim that Pollard's information was passed to the Russians. In December 1987, a UPI report quoted U.S. intelligence analysts as saying that some of Pollard's material was "traded to the Soviets in return for promises to increase emigration of Soviet Jews to Israel."

On August 7th, 1985, more than three months before Jonathan Pollard was arrested, the *Intelligence Digest* newsletter ran a story under the title: "Israeli espionage in the Pentagon." It stated: "While a seemingly continuous stream of espionage scandals shakes the U.S. intelligence community and has done and is doing incalculable harm to American and Western security, a major cover-up of alleged Israeli espionage is being conducted by high-level Pentagon officials. Washington observers claim this cover-up makes Watergate appear like child's play.

Unfortunately, it appears that various intelligence passed on to Israel, including high technology secrets, has ended up in the hands of the KGB. This includes high-tech material denied to NATO, but, according to intelligence sources, permitted for transfer to Israel by the authority of pro-Zionist officials in the Pentagon.

All of this was brought to light by the intelligence indiscretion of a Pentagon official and the Israeli Mossad. After the FBI had gathered 600 pages in its file on the case it was suddenly dropped. Intelligence sources say that in the Pentagon the purchase of military equipment from Israel has been expedited, and high technology items continue to be sent to Israel while the transfer of some of the same items to NATO nations is being denied. Interestingly enough, some of the material passed on to Israel has found its way to Moscow. NATO counter--intelligence is now investigating the possibility of a compromised U.S. origin for high technology secrets found in Soviet KGB possession when French security agents cracked a Soviet intelligence ring in Paris. Known as the "Paris Papers" case it was first believed that the high-tech material might have been passed on to the Soviets from a NATO nation. It was later learned, however, that the classified papers reached the KGB from Israel.

It has been known for some time, but withheld from the American public due to Zionist Lobby pressure, that Israel has been sharing various intelligence matters with the Soviet Union- including information exchanges on Nazi war criminals and leading European anti-communists of the World War II era and early post-war era. Israel has also provided intelligence favors for Moscow to obtain release, and better treatment, for Jews within the Soviet bloc."

The proof may again be in the pudding. Jewish refusnik Natan Sharansky was released in February 1986, just a few months after Pollard was caught. By the fall of 1989 a massive exodus of Soviet Jews had begun. It isn't hard to believe that Shamir took this very valuable strategic information and, concluding that it might not be good for Israel to be so firmly in America's sphere of influence, bartered with it with the Russians. It certainly would not have been the first (or last) time Israel would trade arms or intelligence information for Jews.

CLAIM: Ben Menashe told me in April 1991 that Robert McFarlane was recruited by Rafi Eitan to be an "Israeli agent" and that he was the infamous Mr. X in the Pollard case, a high ranking official who told Pollard which documents to steal. He said William Odom, a former head of the National Security Agency, suspected McFarlane's "special relationship" with Israel and wanted to expose it but that the Administration felt it would be better if McFarlane just resigned.

Claiming that McFarlane was an Israeli agent was potentially the most explosive of all of Ben Menashe's assertions. Martin Kilian of *Der Spiegel* remarked to me: "If this turns out to be true, the shit is going to hit the fan in American-Israel relations."

FACT: Robert (Bud) McFarlane was by far Israel's strongest supporter in the Administration. For instance, on numerous occasions he tried to delay arms sales to Saudi Arabia. In early 1985, for instance, he clashed with Secretary of State George Schultz and Secretary of State Caspar Weinberger who were pushing for massive arms sales to Saudi Arabia and Jordan.

According to one of his aides, McFarlane told them: "We've got lots of fights on the Hill first- the MX missile, aid to the Contras, arms control, the defense budget- and the Middle East is fifth. If the Arabs complain, lay it off on me, say the White House wants the review." (*New York Times Magazine*, May 26th, 1985)

McFarlane was also the major White House backer of the Iraqi pipeline deal. To be built by the Bechtel company it would feed 300,000 barrels of oil each day from Iraqi oil fields to a terminal at the Jordanian port of Aquaba. As part of the arrangement, then Israeli Prime Minister Shimon Peres's Labour party would receive up to $1 billion over a ten year period in return for a pledge not to bomb the pipeline in the event of a war.

Originally, it may have been intended to have this money come from the Pentagon's budget.

When John Poindexter took over from McFarlane as National Security Adviser in December 1985 he killed a plan his predecessor had come up with to have secret payments made to Israel from a heavily disguised National Security Council- controlled appropriation in the Pentagon's budget. (*Washington Post*, March 5th, 1988) "The idea was for it to come out of the defence budget on an installment basis," one source was quoted as saying. "It was to be a payment to the Israelis to be good." (*Washington Post*, February 25th, 1988)

It may be nothing but coincidence, but Israel's spy in Washington, Jonathan Pollard, was operating throughout McFarlane's period as National Security Advisor. A month after Pollard was arrested, McFarlane resigned. Yet six months later he is leading a delegation on a secret mission to Teheran. Why didn't National Security Adviser Poindexter go?

McFarlane's ties to Rafi Eitan, then the Prime Minister's Anti-Terrorism Advisor, and later named as the Israeli intelligence agent behind the Pollard affair, also need to be investigated.

Ben Menashe gave a sworn affidavit to Inslaw Inc., a Washington, D.C. computer company whose PROMIS software for intelligence agencies was stolen by Earl Brian, a friend of former Attorney General Edwin Meese. He says that in 1982 Eitan told him that he had received a copy of the PROMIS program from Earl Brian and former National Security Adviser Robert McFarlane. Another intelligence source told me that in 1982 Eitan teamed-up with McFarlane to find a way for Israel to "view" a security report the President receives on his desk every morning.

Of all those involved with the Contra supply effort and arms sales to Iran, McFarlane paid the heaviest price. Why was he made the scapegoat? Could it be that the rest of the Administration knew of his "special relationship" with Israel? When he resigned Iran Contra was still a secret. Did someone like Bush say to him "Bud, how would you like to be charged with treason? This is what we want you to do: lay low for a while, if what we're doing ever becomes known we're going to need you to take the rap." When it did and McFarlane was called before Congress he supposedly tried to kill himself with an overdose of Vallium. Was this truly by accident?

After a while one starts to believe what Ben Menashe has to say, if for no other reason than that his information is too accurate to be simply fabricated. For instance, he described an incident to me which I later found, after a lot of searching, reported in *The New York Times*.

French Prime Minister Jacques Chirac was quoted as saying that senior West German officials believed Israel to have masterminded an attempted terrorist plot in April 1986, to blow up an Israeli jet in England. Both Helmut Kohl and Hans Deitrich Genscher said that they didn't believe Syria was behind the incident. The plot to blow up the El Al plane, they claimed, was carried out by Israeli secret service agencies with the help of renegades within the Syrian secret service who wanted to embarrass Assad. Britain broke off relations with Syria over the affair. A Jordanian citizen, Nezar Hindawio, was given a 45 year sentence for trying to smuggle explosives hidden in his pregnant girlfriend's suitcase. (*New York Times*, November 8th, 1986)

Israel obviously wouldn't blow up its own plane, but by "discovering" the bomb, it certainly did embarrass Syria while reaping heaps of praise for Israeli security methods. Ben Menashe could have read the report in a newspaper as I did. On the other hand, he could have been a part of it or seen it in Israeli intelligence files.

What Was Ben Menashe's Agenda?

Who is Ari Ben Menashe? The most logical answer would be that he began working as a low-level translator in the Israeli intelligence services, moved up a few grades over time, and by 1985 was sent to London to coordinate arms deals as part of the Joint Committee's activities. By 1986 or 1987 he had stepped on a few toes and was thrown out.

Acting as an independent freelancer, he carried out tasks here and there for someone in Prime Minister Shamir's office; activities that even the Israeli intelligence services might not have known about. During this time he met a lot of people in the arms business and tried to put together a few deals. However without the backing of a country or alot of money, he didn't get very far. He probably stepped on a few more toes and someone in Israel set him up for trying to sell the C-130 planes.

After spending more than a year in jail he got out, very bitter, and wanting to get back at Israel. He realized that exposing only Israeli covert operations was not going to get him a big fat book contract. To attract the attention of the press, he started talking about the covert operations of the Reagan and Bush administrations.

Regardless of how many articles come out trashing him, the information Ben Menashe provided was too good for him to be dismissed simply as a charlatan. I assumed he acquired his knowledge from Israeli intelligence files. That's good enough for me. Unlike the mainstream press,

I never expected him to hand over documents proving beyond a shadow of a doubt that the Reagan-Bush White House was filled with media manipulation, disinformation, deceit and corruption. Yet the way the mainstream press attacked him, it was if Ben Menashe's credibility, not the information he was offering, was the issue. Nearly every single article painted him as untrustworthy instead of analyzing the possibility that the events he was describing had taken place.

The last I heard from Ben Menashe was in November 1991 when he phoned my answering machine in New York and left three messages for me in a span of twenty minutes. It reminded me of the first time I met him. He was on his way to Australia and he told me he would call me when he got there. Why, he didn't tell me. Sure enough the moment he landed he phoned me (I called the airlines to find out when the plane landed. He must have made the call in the airport lobby on the way to retrieving his baggage).

This was the way Ari attracted journalists. He befriended them. He made them feel important. He gave them the impression he was going to reveal everything to them. And he did a good job. He had me hanging on his every word and flying half way across the country just to spend a few hours with him.

Ben Menashe was my passport into the secret

world of covert operations. Each time I would walk away from meeting him it would be like stepping out of another dimension, crossing over from the covert to the overt world.

As a writer on Israeli and Arab affairs I had believed myself quite knowledgeable about Middle East and American-Israel subjects. Ben Menashe made me realize how little I really knew. Contrary to the disinformation the American and Israeli governments had planted, what I thought was reality wasn't real at all. What Bush and Shamir said no longer mattered. It was what went on in the covert world that was important.

Ari Ben Menashe made me understand that disinformation is the name of the game. It doesn't matter what a government does, only what the public thinks it is doing.

Beyond the Pale:
The True Nature of
American-Israeli Relations

The trouble with understanding the true nature of American-Israel relations is that the subject is cluttered up with a lot of misinformation. The "conventional wisdom" in Middle East policy circles, in all camps, is misguided as to what really moves American-Israel relations because it does not consider the covert aspect of this relationship. Essentially, that is what this book is about.

However, even if we remain in the overt world, the "conventional wisdom" never gets the story right. For instance, in the early 1980's the combination of being pro-Israel and anti-Communist was a very powerful one. You could get to the same position by considering Israel an important strategic asset or by being anti-Soviet.

However the "Israel is a strategic asset of America" argument may have been nothing more than an election gimmick and a cover for the Administration's true intentions in the Middle East. William Quandt, a senior fellow at the Brookings Institute and a former aid to Zbigniew Brzezinski, says that Reagan was the first American politician to refer to Israel as a strategic ally of the U.S. that could be counted on to fight communist intrusion into the Middle East.

"Until then one would have had a hard time finding senior U.S. officials using that type of language," Quandt claims. "No one in Carter's administration thought like that."

There's no doubt that Reagan himself was pro-Israel, some say instinctively pro-Israel. Former ambassador to Saudi Arabia Robert Neuman attributes these sentiments to Reagan's idealistic vision of Israel and to the many Jewish friends he had in Hollywood.

Yet it's doubtful whether it was Reagan who was orchestrating American foreign policy in the Middle East and conducting relations with Israel. Neuman says Reagan had little penchant for these subjects. "When you briefed Reagan on Middle East politics or relations with Israel like I did during the 1980 campaign and during his presidency, you would watch as his eyes would glaze over. There was no point in going into too many details."

What mattered was not what the actual policies of the Administration were, but what the American public thought they were. As a majority of the American public has always been predisposed to Israel instead of the Arabs, from the 1980 Presidential campaign through the two Reagan administrations, it was politically astute for the Reagan White House to be identified and perceived as being pro-Israel.

However, while Israeli leaders and pro-Israel lobbyists in the U.S. relished the thought that they now had a President who viewed them as America's number one ally in the region, they were in fact being hoodwinked. Far from being considered a "strategic asset", in the minds of those who carried any serious weight with the President, Israel was a "strategic liability". Just below the surface another sphere of the Reagan White House's attitudes towards Israel existed, a world of secret agendas and foreign policies carried out behind the backs of Congress.

The Reagan Administration's presiding policy towards Israel was based on the "level battlefield doctrine" (LBD) and designed to weaken Israel. The White House was then (and still is today) more interested in a steady flow of Middle East oil and multi-billion dollar sales of U.S. arms to the region than in Israel's security. The Saudis can fulfill both of these needs- Israel, neither.

The LBD became the cornerstone of U.S. policy towards Israel. The doctrine is based on a Saudi Arabian notion that the problem in the Middle East is not with the Arabs, but in Israel's reckless use of its military superiority. The administration must ensure that the Arabs achieve a parity with Israel militarily, so that Israel will be pressured into concessions which will lead to a comprehensive Middle East peace.

The doctrine expressed itself in the view that if Iran won its war with Iraq it might "consume" Saudi Arabia and Kuwait and thus jeopardize American access to Middle East oil. This explains why the White House began supporting Iraq sometime between 1982 and 1983. The Saudis also had another reason for urging America to support Iraq. The LBD said that a strong Iraqi regime would be an effective balance against Israel so that Israel wouldn't "feel so strong" and thus, as suggested above, would be more flexible in the peace process.

Conservative ideologue Irving Kristol says that while Reagan was pro-Israel from the very beginning, Bush and Baker were not. "There was no reason to expect that they would be," he says. "They had always dealt with Arabs, not Jews."

When he became President not much was known about George Bush's attitude towards the Middle East. It may have been influenced by the views of his fellow Bonesmen (Bush was inducted into the Skull and Bones secret society while a student at Yale University). Another possible influence were President Harry Truman's foreign policy advisers George Marshall, Dean Acheson, and Robert Lovett. All three were reportedly against U.S. support for the establishment of the State of Israel, believing it would pose a threat to U.S. hegemony over access to Mideast oil. Lovett was heard to have said that "Israel was one ally too many."(*The Wise Men: Six Friends and the World They Made*, by Walter Isaacson and Evan Thomas, Simon and Schuster New York 1986)

Far from being pro-Israel, the Reagan years were rife with anti-Israel actions with then Vice President Bush leading the anti-Israel caucus in the White House. Despite Israel being lauded as America's "strategic ally" in the region, there really weren't many instances where the administration backed Israel politically against the Arabs. While it is former Secretary of Defence Caspar Weinberger who was always thought of as being the most anti-Israel, some say anti-Semitic, of all of Reagan's cabinet, that perception may have camouflaged Bush's hostility to Israel.

Weinberger denies that he was anti-Israel. "While I was Secretary of Defence cooperation between the military of Israel and the U.S. was never closer," he told me in March 1991. "Former

Prime Minister Shimon Peres and Defence Minister Moshe Arens told me ties between the two countries were never stronger. During the Reagan administration we tried to strengthen the Israeli alliance, and without any question we did. While there were occasions when I had difficulties with Israeli policies, overall the relationship was very positive."

Yet whenever the Administration came crashing down hard on Israel, Bush seemed to be leading the assault. For instance, when Israeli jets bombed Iraq's nuclear reactor in 1981, columnist William Safire wrote that "Bush led the initiative to punish Israel by withholding shipments of previously promised F-16 aircraft." (*Jerusalem Post*, November 11th, 1988)

Former Secretary of State Alexander Haig says that in the Cabinet discussion that followed the bombing raid, Bush demanded that the U.S. cut off all aid to Israel, economic and military, because of what Bush described as an "outrageous" breach of international law. (*Israel Army Radio*, December 28th, 1991)

Haig also claims that Bush convinced Reagan to support a UN resolution condemning Israel for its invasion of Lebanon in 1982. During the June 1985 hijacking of a TWA plane by Shiite fundamentalists, Bush said that "all people held against international law should be released" — an obvious reference to Lebanese prisoners then being held by Israel. During the initial investigation into the Iran Contra scandal, Bush told the Tower Commission that U.S. foreign policy was "in the grip of the Israelis." (*Jerusalem Post*, November 11th, 1988)

Secretary of State James Baker's views about Israel weren't much more positive than Bush's. Morris Amitay, a former executive director of AIPAC, remembers that during the height of the AWACs debate, Baker told him that the pro-Israel opposition to the sale was "simply hurting U.S. relations with moderate Arabs."

Says Amitay: "I did not get a very good feeling about his viewing Israel as an important strategic asset during that conversation," (*The Jerusalem Post*, November 11th, 1988)

The Covert Relationship: The Other Side of American-Israeli Relations

Considering the failure of most Middle East observers to detect the true nature of the overt side of American-Israel relations, it is understandable that these analysts are unfamiliar with the covert side of the story. Hidden from the public's eye, it is rarely discussed or written about in the main-stream press.

What does it consist of? Secret agendas. Covert operations. U.S. policies hidden from the Congress and the American people. Every time the Administration carries out this type of agenda, it is invariably as a result of its relations with Israel or effects upon Israel's security in one way or another.

For instance, America's relationship with Syria since the early days of the Bush White House can be described as one long covert operation, shrouded in mystery. Evidence of a secret deal between the U.S. and Syria resulted in the death of two or three agents who had infiltrated a Palestinian terrorist organization in Syria. The agents reportedly worked either for Israel's Mossad or for another Western intelligence service. They were unmasked because of detailed information which Secretary of State James Baker handed Syrian President Hafez al-Assad and foreign Minister Farouk al-Sharaa during a meeting in Damascus on September 14th, 1990 when the Administration was trying to bring Syria into the coalition against Iraq. (*New York Times*, February 8th, 1991)

Intelligence officials informed the New York Times that they were told in February 1991 that the killings stemmed from American efforts in the summer of 1990 to uncover a plot by Syrian-based terrorists, to assassinate the United States Ambassador to Jordan, Roger G. Harrison.

After Baker's meeting with the Syrians, there was a fierce argument between U.S. intelligence and State Department officials over giving Assad a detailed briefing of U.S. information on Syrian involvement in terrorism. The intelligence agencies in the U.S. were worried that if the State Department confronted Assad with evidence of his country's support for terrorism, it would reveal the intelligence gathering methods of the U.S. as well as compromise agents currently working undercover.

The State Department eventually won and intelligence officials believe that Syria gave the PLO the information obtained from the briefing with Baker and enabled them to identify the undercover agents. In November or December 1990 the U.S. learned that the agents had been killed.

Several Bush administration officials tried to deflect attention away from the affair by insisting that the undercover agents were working for the Jordanian state intelligence service and had infiltrated a Syrian-based Palestinian terrorist group to provide Jordan with information on terrorist activities. The officials said that Jordan shared this information with the CIA. (*New York Times*, March 12th, 1991)

This would be a possible explanation if it were not for the fact that Jordan hasn't been the target of a bomb attack by a Palestinian terrorist group in more than twenty years.

The next part of the secret U.S.-Syrian deal came in Geneva in July 1991 when Bush met Syrian President Hafez al-Assad. Syrian Foreign Minister Farouk al-Sharaa claims Bush made a promise to Damascus that Israel would have to return the Golan Heights. The White House responded with a statement that denied cutting a secret deal with Syria, insisting that Sharaa simply misunderstood Bush. When a reporter asked al-Sharaa if Bush mentioned an Israeli withdrawal on all fronts, he responded, "Yes, yes, and the American administration rejected the annexation of one centimeter of the Golan Heights." (*New York Post*, July 26th, 1991)

When *New York Times* columnist William Safire probed Administration officials about the contents of a letter sent by Assad to Bush after the Geneva meetings, he discovered that "Assad had spelled out his understanding of assurances given to him over the past six weeks from the United States. (*New York Times*, July 18th, 1991)

Another sphere of the secret ties between the U.S. and Syria could be seen in the March 1992 bombing of the Israeli Embassy in Buenos Aires, which left 26 dead and 200 injured. The reasons no one has yet been apprehended for the massacre is that Syria was behind it, not Muslim Fundamentalists, and that the White House pressured Israel not to reveal Syrian responsibility for the bombing.

Just days after the blast, the Argentinean news agency TELAM reported that four men and a woman had been arrested by the federal police anti-terrorist brigade in a raid on a downtown apartment. The Argentinean police said that the raid was connected to the bombing, but gave no further details. The police's press office subsequently denied the report. (*Inside Israel*, April 1993)

The initial investigation was delayed until five and half hours after the blast, by which time much of the evidence had been destroyed in the rescue operation. The official investigation has now been frozen, though its latest theory is that the explosion occurred in the basement of the embassy compound, accusing, by implication, the Israelis, of storing weapons which accidentally exploded.

This is in direct contradiction of the evidence which indicates a suicide bomber. Body parts belonging to a dark-skinned man flew through the window of a doctor living close to the embassy. Ballisitics experts said the force required for these body parts to have been hurled through the window strongly suggests a suicide bomber. Several other corpses remain unidentified to this day.

Israeli investigators who arrived just after the blast reached a very different conclusion. They found the remains of a car inside the embassy compound and traced it to a Pakistani named Abbas Malek who was the personal aide of the Pakistani ambassador. Malek was filmed escaping the blast site minutes after the explosion by Israeli embassy cameras. Two top-ranking Argentinean intelligence officials were given access to the photographs. After the investigation was frozen they leaked the license number of the photographed car to a local TV station's investigation.

Also caught on film was the license plate of the suicide vehicle. It was traced to a car dealer who admitted selling the car three weeks before the blast to an Arab with a Brazilian accent, Ribahru Dahloz, who paid in cash. The dealer demanded a 30% commission, which he was paid partly in banknotes later traded to Syrian banks. Even with this evidence the police did not attempt to apprehend Dahloz.

This was the first hint of a deep Syrian connection to the explosion. On the day of the blast both of the police security guards normally posted outside the Embassy were absent. According to the police, one guard was late while the other was removed by the Israeli ambassador, Yitzhak Shefi, an accusation he vehemently denies. One of the guards previously spent six years posted at the Syrian Embassy.

Argentinean President Carlos Menem was born in Syria. According to Israeli journalist Nurit Steinberg, who lives in Buenos Aires and has investigated the bombing, Menem maintains close ties with members of terrorist groups within the Syrian community. Steinberg gathered dozens of documents confirming these connections and has published the findings of her investigation in a weekly Jerusalem newspaper owned by the prestigious Hebrew daily *Haaretz*.

Her work, however, was not well received. She has been threatened repeatedly, had a grenade thrown at her doorstep, and had her house broken into. Only one object was stolen: the computer diskette containing notes of her investigation.

Menem's wife, Suliema, was born in the Syrian town of Yatrud, also the birthplace of Monzer Al-Kassar, a drug and arms smuggler who has been implicated in the Pan AM 103 bombing and also helped Oliver North supply weapons to the Nicaraguan Contras. Al-Kassar has built a multi-million dollar empire on military deals in Eastern and Western Europe. In July 1987, *The Los Angeles Times* reported that Al-Kassar had clear business links with the Abu Nidal terrorist organization.

Nine months before the embassy blast, a television news report from Damascus showed Menem's brother Munir, at the time his country's ambassador to Syria, deep in conversation with Al-Kassar. Shortly after the bombing he was recalled.

Six months after the attack on the embassy, Al-Kassar was finally apprehended in Spain and put on trial for smuggling explosives to terrorists. The Argentinean government requested his extradition, claiming that he was wanted in Argentina for passport violations. At the trial, Al-Kassar claimed to have received his Argentinean passport directly from Menem and even to have posed for the photo wearing the President's tie.

The Spanish government followed the Argentine request with an extradition order of their own. They wanted Menem's personal secretary, Amira Yuma, to stand trial for being a member of the biggest drug network in Spain. Yuma is Menem's sister-in-law. Argentina, not surprisingly, turned the request down.

In September 1992, Menem sent a message to Jerusalem asking that the Israeli Ambassador to Argentina, Yitzhak Shefi, be recalled. Shefi had publicly attacked Menem, who still maintained that neo-Nazis were behind the bombing. Shefi also accused the Israeli government of not protesting the stalled investigation, adding that perhaps Jerusalem was not really interested in finding out who was behind the blast. He was among the chorus of people who claimed that the investigation was being delayed to prevent a major diplomatic embarrassment both for the Argentineans and the Israelis.

The blast had all the hallmarks of a classic Shiite car bombing. It is also difficult to ignore the timing of the attack. It occurred one month to the day after Israeli forces killed the Syrian-controlled Hizbollah leader, Abbas Musawi, and not long after the last of the American hostages were released from Lebanon.

Musai had more enemies in America than in Israel. In the early 1980's he had planned the attacks on the American Embassy in Beirut and on the Marine barracks compound, the latter of which left 241 servicemen dead. He is also widely believed to have ordered the kidnappings of Americans in Lebanon, including CIA station chief in Beirut, William Buckley.

At a memorial service one year after the Buenos Aires blast, Israeli Foreign Minister Shimon Peres stated that Israel knew who was behind the terrorist act, but would not say who. Everyone assumed Peres meant Iran. However the evidence points directly to Damascus.

Iran-Contra II: Another Arms for Hostage Deal?

Another phase in Bush and Baker's covert Middle East policy was enacted just before the Middle East peace conference in Madrid in October 1991. It was no mere coincidence that the 17 Western hostages were released just before the start of the Madrid conference. The hostages were an embarrassment to Syria. The American public would not be sympathetic to the Arabs as long as there were American hostages being held in Lebanon. The question is what did the U.S. give Syria, and Iran, in return?

Could it have been another arms-for-hostages deal? Iran Contra number two?

Events during the early part of March 1992 may be instrumental in unraveling this mystery. It began when Israeli intelligence services first detected the Dae Hung Ho, a North Korean missile cargo ship loaded with Scud-C ballistic missiles in the Persian Gulf. At the time, the Bush administration was giving the American people the impression that they were leading the battle against the spread of ballistic missiles and their technology to countries which did not already possess them.

On March 7th, 1992, National Security Adviser Brent Scowcroft said "we are concerned about any type of missile proliferation. It is dangerous and destabilizing. We are always considering options." When asked what the Administration was doing to do to deal with the matter, Scowcroft replied: "We are doing what we can." Asked whether the incident over the Korean ships would come to a head soon, Scowcroft replied: "I don't know if it will ever come to a head."

When asked about media reports pointing to the Administration's concern over the matter, Pentagon Spokesperson Pete Williams responded: "my concern is that all of these sources have cranked this thing up to a higher priority than it actually was for the Administration."

Western diplomats said that the progress of the ships was being watched closely and that the U.S. Navy knew exactly where they were. (*International Herald Tribune*, March 10th, 1992)

Yet suddenly the aircraft carrier America and its entire battle group lost sight of the ships. General Joseph Hoar, who succeeded General Norman Schwarzkopf as commander of U.S. Central Command, told the House Armed Services Committee "We were unable to locate that ship, clear and simple."

Previously the Administration had hesitated to intercept and board the ships. Now they it was claiming that it had lost track of them.

Hoar quickly changed the focus of the question by suggesting that it was still unclear what cargo the ship was carrying: "the inability to find the cargo ship has dealt a blow to U.S. intelligence, depriving analysts of the opportunity to obtain details of the freighter's cargo. What we have lost by our failure to pick up that ship is that we would have been able to alert our intelligence colleagues to determine more specifically what was there." (*Washington Post*, March 12th, 1992)

Williams fed the press more nonsense when he claimed: "I can't tell you precisely why we didn't see it all the time. Perhaps it hugged the coast line and wasn't picked out of the heavy coastal traffic in that area."

One Navy official said that initially the ship wasn't a very high priority. "We were told to look for the ship, no more." (*Time*, March 23rd, 1992) Yet the vessels best suited for this task, the aircraft carrier America battle group, were carrying out exercises hundreds of miles away.

Is it possible that the most sophisticated and expensive collection of armed forces in the world simply lost sight of two transport ships? That everyone except the U.S. navy knew what the cargo ship was carrying?

In fact, Israel was reminding the world that the U.S. wasn't doing anything about the North Korean ships. They let the cat out of the bag.

The Administration was carrying out a secret

policy to supply Iran and Syria with SCUD missiles but Israeli intelligence got in the way. Embarrassed and mad as hell, the Administration decided to teach Israel a lesson. In a classic case of media manipulation, *The Washington Times* published a story quoting Administration officials and claiming that Israel gave a Patriot missile to China. Reports in other publications followed, purporting that Israel has systematically transferred or sold American weaponry or technology to third-parties without the required permission.

Whether these reports are true or false is irrelevant to understanding the covert agenda taking place. If the reports are false then it is nothing but a smear campaign against Israel. Even then, Israel loses because nobody believes Israel would admit to it even if they had done it.

Assuming for argument's sake they are true, if the Administration wanted to go public with this information, why did they not simply call a press conference and make an official statement? If the White House is mad as hell at Israel, why can't it come out and say so? Why have "undisclosed sources" release the story?

If the Administration had truly discovered that Israel was transferring American-made weapons to third-world countries, wouldn't the logical response have been to take a senior Israeli official aside and tell him in the sternest manner, "what you did is reprehensible and you will pay a heavy price", then to leave it at that? What does the Administration have to gain by having the affair splashed over the headlines?

All fingers point to a pre-conceived, orchestrated attempt either to smear Israel, or punish Israel, depending on whether Israel was guilty or not. It could not have been merely a coincidence that this information was released only days after the Administration told the American public that the U.S. Navy "lost" a ship it was tracking. If so, was the Administration planning on leaking this information anyway? Was it also a coincidence that these reports hit the press on the eve of Israeli Defence Minister Moshe Arens' visit to the U.S.?

By having the media focus on the question of Israel having transferred American weapons, public attention was deflected from the Administration's failure to intercept the North Korean ships. It took about one day for the American public to completely forget the ships. The technique is a perfect way of clearing damaging or embarrassing incidents from the press. You wipe out one news item by replacing it with an even bigger story. Disinformation and illusion were the name of the game in the Bush White House.

If Israel was guilty, why would the Administration have acted in the way that it did? Would the White House necessarily have wanted the world to know that Israel had double crossed them and was not to be trusted? How could the Administration not cut all aid and sales of weapons to Israel after such a breach of trust by an ally?

One possible scenario is that Israel knew of the North Korean ships and of the arms deals with Syria and Iran, and told Bush and Baker "if the loan guarantees aren't approved we'll let the cat out of the bag." At that point, Bush might have said, "just try, and see what will happen."

Why would the Administration want Syria and Iran to have improved SCUD missiles? Because America is still trading arms for hostages. Either before or after the Persian Gulf War it made secret deals with both Syria and Iran.

One sign of a deal was the $278 million the Iranians received from America. The Administration claimed that this was a coincidence and that the money that was turned over to the Iranians was "the outcome of arbitrations dating from 1981". (Iran was seeking an out-of-court settlement of its claim for $12 billion that it says the late Shah paid for arms that were never delivered.) What a remarkable coincidence! A debt of ten years' standing is repaid at just the same time that the hostages are being released! While the American people were being fed this version, Teheran

Radio said that part of the agreement included a non-retaliation pledge from the U.S. (*Newsweek*, December 16th, 1991)

Was it also by chance that Syria and Iran organized the hostage release when it was these same two countries who took delivery of the SCUDs?

Just as in the first Iran-Contra, the Americans wanted their hostages back and were willing to trade arms to get them released. In fact, it may have been a new way for the Administration to secretly arm countries: providing weapons by not reacting.

In the middle of this secret policy, however, as usual, a facet of the covert American-Israeli relationship was being played out. Without understanding this side of bi-lateral relations between the two countries, one can't be sure what America's actual policy in the Middle East really is.

America and Iraq Versus Israel

The Reagan and Bush Administrations' policy of supporting and arming Saddam Hussein was part of the White House's Level Battlefield Doctrine(LBD) whereby Iraq was used as a counterweight to Israel's military superiority in the region.

The genesis of this relationship goes back to March 1982 when then CIA director William Casey is reported to have made a secret trip to Baghdad and arranged for Iraq to be removed from the State Department's list of states supporting terrorism, a prerequisite for the subsequent restoration of diplomatic relations. Then Vice-President Bush himself acted as an intermediary in delivering strategic military advice to Saddam Hussein. (*Los Angeles Times*, May 7th, 1992)

By taking Iraq off the State Department's list of nations which support terrorism, it enabled the sale of so-called "dual use" items which although ostensibly sold for civilian purposes would have an actual use on the battlefield. As one former senior State Department official put it: "The decision to help Iraq was not a CIA rogue initiative. The policy was researched at the State Department and approved at the highest levels." (*New York Times*, January 26th, 1992)

The Bush Administration tried to cover up its role in arming Saddam Hussein by having the "conventional wisdom" gurus argue that the policy was simply geopolitical - to ensure that Iran didn't win the Iran-Iraq War. However this fails to take into account the fact that the effort to arm Saddam Hussein increased, in some areas dramatically, after Iran and Iraq agreed to a ceasefire in August 1988.

What we know of this secret policy comes from information the Israeli government leaked to reporters in June 1990, before the Gulf War. In the hush-hush, covert world slugfest that Bush was having with Yitzhak Shamir from the moment of Bush's inauguration, the entire Iraqgate scandal, including illegal loans to Iraq from the Italian bank BNL, only became public because of deliberate Israeli leaks.

Despite the fact that U.S. export law forbade these third-party transfers of American-made weapons, neither Vice nor President Bush, nor anyone else in the Administration, made any effort to stop them.

According to classified State Department cables dated late in the summer of 1986, Saudi Arabia shipped an undisclosed number of American-made Mk-84 2,000 pound bombs to Iraq. Sources in the Bush Administration were quoted in *The Los Angeles Times* on May 7th, 1982 saying that these Saudi transfers were carried out with the full approval of the U.S. government.

Secretary of State James Baker called the transfers "inadvertent" and claimed that they had been duly brought to the attention of Congress. When President Bush was asked whether the previous administration had authorized these transfers from Saudi Arabia to Syria in April 1992, he gave his trademark response: "No. The answer to your question is no."

Complications began to arise for the administration by the end of 1984 when Iraq was holding negotiations to purchase 45 Bell helicopters which were to have multi-mission capabilities. Senator Alan Dixon, a Democrat from Illinois, voiced his opposition to the Commerce Department over an export license, yet the sale went through.

By January 1985, the acquisition of U.S. arms by Iraq increased dramatically. American M-60 tanks, heavy artillery, concussion bombs and bridging equipment were among the equipment used by Iraq to push Iranian troops out of the Hawr al-Hammar swamp north of Basra. One report said that "if relations continue to improve, and if Hussein leads his country to a pro-Western tilt, the Americans may consider selling him F-15 and F-16 aircraft." (*Foreign Report*, October 1st, 1985)

U.S.-Iraqi military cooperation certainly improved. The Kuwaiti newspaper Al Wattan said on January 28th, 1985 that "discussions by Iraq on acquiring 45 American fighter planes began in November 1984, in addition to sophisticated radar units and special anti-aircraft missiles." The report said that military attaches had recently been exchanged between the U.S. and Iraq and that the head of the Iran-Iraq desk at the U.S. Defence Department toured the front speaking with high ranking Iraqi officers.

In August 1985, Hughes announced the sale of 24 Model 530F commercial utility helicopters to Iraq's Ministry of Communications and Transportation. On August 26th, 1985, Hatsav, the Iraqi press agency, reported that 150 Iraqi pilots were being trained at United States Air Force bases in the Turkish city of Dierbakher near the Iraqi border, and that NATO was supervising the training. On November 17th, 1986, Hatsav reported similar training exercises at Diar in Turkey. In August, *Newsweek* claimed that there were civil technicians from the U.S. airforce in Iraq training Iraqi pilots.

The Administration also allowed Iraq to acquire key military technology. In late 1992 former Under-Secretary of Commerce Dennis Kloske told the House Foreign Affairs Subcommittee on International Economic Policy and Trade that the State Department in particular disregarded his recommendation to limit the flow of American technology to Iraq because the Administration wanted to encourage better relations with Baghdad.

Despite the fact that the U.S. was a signatory to the Missile Technology Control Regime (MTCR) — an international monitoring system aimed at countries with the potential for developing nuclear missiles - licenses for the transfer of U.S. missile technology for the Saad 16 project were approved. On June 8th, 1990, Kloske sent a proposal to deputy CIA director Robert Gates, outlining the expanded application of the MTCR to exports to Iraq. Gates turned the plan down. (*Commonweal*, June 14th, 1991)

Throughout this period Israel had known about these military sales and technology transfer through its monitoring of the activities of Chilean arms dealer Carlos Carduen who maintained a special relationship with the CIA. In late 1991 ABC *News Nightline* conducted an investigation of how the CIA knew about transfers of cluster bomb technology from a Pennsylvania company that shipped these weapons, to arms stockpiles in Iraq. The bombs, which scatter tiny bomblets over a wide area, were particularly suited to Iraq's unskilled air force.

Also included in the report was a story on a company in Boca Raton, Florida, that helped Libya build its Rafta chemical weapons facility. It was able to do so with the full cooperation of CIA contracted shippers who transferred the deadly armaments to Libya and Iraq. The White House denied there were any arms sales to Iraq, and that Mr. Gates ever met with Cardeun.

The primary source for the story was Richard Babayan. Babayan, who is originally from Iran, says that under Gates' command, he transported arms to Iraq. Babayan testified in a closed House subcommittee hearing about arms sales to Iraq. He swore in an affidavit that in March 1991 he attended a series of meetings arranged by Gates in order to ship arms to Iraq via the Chilean arms dealer, Carlos Carduen.

When the Iran-Iraq war broke out in 1980, Carlos Carduen, then a small Santiago arms manufacturer, had contacts with Iraqi army officers interested in obtaining cluster bomb technology. Carduen defended his arms sales to Hussein by reminding his critics that he began selling Iraq weapons: "When Iraq was considered a friend of the West fighting the Ayatollah Khomeini." (*Time*, December 10th, 1990)

Babayan's family, owners of a prominent Iranian shipping company, were the sole shippers of arms to the Shah until his ouster in 1979. Babayan claims he was an asset for Iranian intelligence, and hired by the CIA in 1979 as part of an attempt to topple the Khomeini regime and free the 52 American hostages. (*The Boca Raton News*, July 7th, 1991)

Babayan claims to have worked for the CIA throughout the 1980s as a troubleshooter and to have begun working in 1984 on a CIA operation out of Geneva to create an arms pipeline to Iraq.

Babayan was put in charge of opening bank accounts and chartering ships to transfer the weapons. He says the arms came from NATO stockpiles in Belgium and West Germany, and from South Africa and Latin America. Babayan contends that he chartered ships from Greece and Liberia and transferred the arms from the ports of Antwerp and Rotterdam to the Iraqi port of Basra and the Jordanian port of Aqaba. From there they were transported over land to Iraq. Payment was made in form of Iraqi oil sales profits diverted to Swiss bank accounts. (*Boca Raton News*, July 2nd 1991; *In These Times*, October 9th, 1991)

Says Babayan: "Despite all the bans and restrictions on him, Saddam was able to obtain the best military equipment, and 95% of it was U.S. equipment. You've got to ask yourself how he circumvented all these arms export barriers. And the answer is, the CIA had to have helped. I know because I was involved in it."

Did the U.S. Help Saddam Hussein Gain Nuclear Capabilities?

An even more frightening question is to what extent did the Bush Administration assist Saddam Hussein's goal of building a nuclear bomb? According to UN Experts, the Iraqi leader was no more than 24 months away from acquiring nuclear weapons capability at the outset of the Gulf War. Government sources in Israel say that while Israel was aware of this campaign, it was unable to stop it.

In the five years before the Gulf War, the Commerce Department licensed more than $1.5 billion worth of sensitive American exports to Iraq, many of which were used at Saddam's nuclear weapons project at al Atheer.

Gary Milhollin, who directs the University of Wisonsin's Project on Nuclear Arms Control, an organization that tracks nuclear exports and the spread of nuclear weapons, says that in August 1989 the Pentagon and Department of Energy invited three Iraqi scientists to a "detonation conference" in Portland, Oregon, which assembled experts from around the world. The Iraqi scientists received information on how to produce shock waves in any configuration, on HMX (the high explosive of choice for nuclear detonation), and on flyer plates (the devices that produce the type of shock waves required to ignite A-bombs). The conference was financed by U.S. taxpayers. (*New York Times*, March 8th, 1992)

In April 1992, the House Committee on Energy and Commerce headed by Congressman John Dingell (D-Michigan) heard testimony from A. Bryan Siebert Jr., the Energy Department's leading authority on the spread of nuclear weapons and head of the Department's Office of Classification and Technology Policy section. After receiving information that Iraq was purchasing parts used in nuclear industries, fuel making equipment and weapon triggers, he urged that export controls be strengthened.

On April 15th, 1989, Siebert, his deputy Roger Heusser, and two aides wrote a memo to Energy Secretary James Watkins describing the evidence they had indicating that Iraq was building an atomic bomb. They recommended that Secretary of State James Baker review the issue in the National Security Council. They wrote: "The pattern of purchases suggested the Iraqis had detailed knowledge of design for building gas centrifuges, which are key to enriching uranium for a bomb's explosive core." Siebert also detailed how Baghdad was attempting to purchase from CSI Technologies, a San Marcos, California company, the palm size capacitators needed to trigger a nuclear bomb.

That memo was also given to Siebert's boss, the Deputy Assistant Secretary for Security Affairs, F. Charles Gilbert, who then sent it to Robert Walsh, the Deputy Assistant Secretary for Intelligence. Walsh told Dingell's committee that at the time he felt the warning was "overstated" and that his department was "uncomfortable with a secretarial level initiative." (*Washington Post*, April 20th, 1992)

He believed that a nuclear weapons program in Iraq "had not been identified" and that while recently purchased items may have nuclear uses they also had "peaceful applications." Walsh claimed that Iraq's level of uranium enrichment technology was believed to be, "at best, in an early state of development." (*New York Times*, April 23rd, 1992)

Dingell called the Department of Energy's failure to heed the warning "a major government failure." Yet that explanation may be somewhat simplistic.

In March 1992 when Israel was thought to have transferred Patriot missile technology to China, an investigation was opened and subsequently closed within 30 days, finding no evidence to back up the claim. If the Energy Department had received these crucial warnings about Iraq's nuclear ambitions, why were they not immediately investigated in the same manner? Lackadaisical attitudes among government officials are just too simplistic an answer.

Sam Gejdenson, a Connecticut Democrat who headed a House Foreign Affairs subcommittee investigation of the exports of sensitive U.S. technology to Iraq, claimed that these sales were not made because the Commerce Department's export control system "broke down" but rather because U.S. foreign policy was to assist the regime of Saddam Hussein. (*New York Times*, January 26th, 1992)

The same intentions may have been behind the Bush Administration's policy in arming Saddam Hussein with nuclear weapons.

How the White House Financed the Iraqi Arms Build-Up

Helping Iraq fight Iran and build its war machine required billions of dollars, money which the Administration couldn't simply go to Congress and ask for. AIPAC, for one, would never have agreed. Instead, the covert operation rested on three pillars: the granting of loan guarantees from the Export-Import Bank, loans from the Atlanta branch of the Banca Nazionale Del Lavoro, and the transfer of military and other technologies.

Had the American people learned of these efforts, there would have been a massive outcry in Congress. However, since they were carried out in secret, that wasn't a problem. To keep the policy secret, the President signed National Security Directive number 26 which is believed to have ordered "pursuit of improved economic and political ties with Iraq."

The Commodity Credit Corporation (CCC) operated two export credit programs in the early days of the Reagan administration to increase U.S. exports of grain to Third World nations. Credit was given by private banks, but guaranteed by the U.S. government. Since the program began, more than $32 billion worth of sales were underwritten.

Due to the Iran-Iraq War, by 1983 there were severe food shortages in Iraq. The renewal of diplomatic ties with the U.S. enabled Iraq to acquire $364 million in U.S. loan guarantees for the purchase of food supplies. From 1983 until the Gulf War, more than $5 billion of Iraqi food purchases were guaranteed by the U.S. government through the program. The American taxpayer got stuck with $2 billion of loans that Iraq left unpaid.

The CCC program solved the State Department's problem of how to increase foreign aid without having to face opposition in Congress. Although only in existence for less than a decade, the loan guarantees program has been transformed from a dull export-enhancement strategy into a foreign policy tool of the Administration. Credit risks took a back seat to the Administration's geopolitical policies. (*Special Report Commissioned by the Simon Wiesenthal Center from Middle East Defence News*)

For instance, at various times in the mid-1980's the Export-Import bank was hesitant to loan Iraq more money because of Saddam's tremendous war debts, which by August 1988 had grown to more than $90 billion (one and half times Iraq's Gross National Product). It did, however, due to the tremendous political pressure put on it by senior Reagan and Bush Administration officials.

Yet in April 1991 John Macomber, then president of the Export-Import Bank, told a Congressional investigation that these two Administrations had exerted no pressure on the Bank to grant guarantees for $267 million in American exports to Iraq from 1987 to 1991. He said "The test is credit worthiness. As far as we were concerned they had brought themselves up to date." (*New York Times*, April 18th, 1991)

Even after the extent of the Iraqi debt became known, the Bush Administration approved an additional $500 million in new credit. In February 1992, a special report in *The Los Angeles Times* revealed that Bush personally signed the secret order to grant a billion dollars in loan guarantees to Iraq nine months before Saddam's forces marched into Kuwait. In 1989 Bush approved a presidential order granting Iraq guarantees against the opposition of the Dept. of Agriculture who warned that the new assistance would enable Saddam to acquire military weapons. The paper claimed that Secretary of State James Baker personally intervened in the affair and ordered Agricultural Secretary Clayton Yeutter to grant the loans.

As early as 1987 the United States Department of Agriculture (USDA) began receiving, and ignoring, warnings that American companies were being asked to ship military goods along with agricultural products. The attempt by the Administration to pressure the USDA and CCC to grant loan guarantees to Iraq was part of a policy to covertly funnel U.S. aid to Iraq.

Says Charlie Rose, a Democrat from North Carolina, "This was done to avoid offending Congress. They didn't want to directly ship military systems to Iraq which would have excited Israel. Nor could they ask Congress to grant foreign aid or military sales credit. So they told the USDA to be as generous as it could with agricultural credits." (*Washington Monthly*, April 1991)

The policy to support Iraq with loan guarantees ran right up to the highest levels of the White House. For instance, in October 1989 Secretary of State James Baker called then Secretary of Agriculture Clayton Yeutter and urged him to approve $1 billion in agricultural loan guarantees to Iraq, explaining that "the CCC program is important to improve and expand our relationship with Iraq, as ordered by the President in NSD-26." (*Los Angeles Times*, March 22nd, 1992). (Although the existence of the NSD is widely known, former President Bush refused to provide a copy of it to Congressional investigators, claiming "executive privilege.")

Even when Congress levied limited sanctions against Iraq after the gassing of Kurdish villages in northern Iraq, which would have prohibited further bank financing without a presidential waiver, the White House wrote a waiver and President Bush signed it on January 17th, 1990 explaining that a prohibition on loan guarantees for Iraq "would not be in the national interest of the United States." (*Los Angeles Times*, March 22nd, 1992)

Why was it so vital for the national interest of the United States for Iraq to receive these loans? If the Bush Administration knew that there were widespread corruption and extortion attempts involved in these loans, why did it insist on approving another billion dollars worth of them?

In fact, for nearly two years before Saddam invaded Kuwait, the Bush Administration seems to have been aware that Iraq was diverting food purchased under the loan guarantees program and exchanging it for money and arms.

In October 1989 a team of investigators from the Department of Agriculture confronted Iraqi officials with these charges. The Agricultural officials were amazed to discover that instead of ending the aid program, the Bush Administration had sought to expand it.

Documents which were published in *The New York Times* on April 27th, 1992, reveal that a number of Soviet block countries, in addition to Jordan and Turkey, aided Iraq in the diversions, and that nuclear technology may also been bartered to Iraq in return for food. The Department of Agriculture's Inspector General said at a meeting with officials of the Commodity Credit Corporation at the Agriculture Department on October 13th, 1989, that diverted funds were used to procure nuclear-related equipment, particularly a "nuclear fuel compounder" and a "nose cone burr."

Nearly one full year before Saddam invaded Kuwait, on April 4th, 1989, a team of Federal and State investigators invaded the Atlanta offices of the Italian state-owned Banca Nazionale del Lavoro (BNL) and demanded to see allegedly secret files which contained information of the bank's "off-the-book" loans to Iraq, recorded in "grey book" accounts.

That raid might never have taken place had it not been for Israel's campaign against the White House's policy of financing Saddam's army.

Two Israeli intelligence sources I have interviewed and an FBI agent who worked in the FBI office in Atlanta claim that information was leaked to the FBI office by the Israeli government in order to put an end to the White House's policy of financing the Iraqi arms build-up.

Initially, the head office of the bank in Rome had claimed that BNL's North American headquarters in New York, which had a $500,000 lending limit, had not authorized the loans.

To head off any inquiry, BNL Chairman Nerio Nesi and its President Giacome Pedde resigned.

In testimony before the Italian Senate in December 1989, Italian Treasury Minister Guido Carli revealed that the credit requests for Iraq were "routinely" channeled to Atlanta by BNL branches in Italy and by the credit and finance departments of the BNL headquarters in Rome. He estimated that of the $2.867 billion in outlays BNL Atlanta had made, $1.017 billion went directly to the Central Bank of Iraq, $781 million to the Rafidain Bank of Baghdad, and the rest to cover letters of credit to other banks and customers. More than $4 billion in unauthorized loans and credit extensions went to finance Iraq's missile and chemical weapons projects. (*Special Report commissioned by the Simon Wiesenthal Center from Middle East Defence News*)

Says Italian Senator Francesco Forte, a member of a parliamentary commission that investigated BNL's affairs: "It was widely known in Italy that the way to finance operations with Iraq was through Atlanta." (*Time*, June 11th, 1990)

Drogoul reportedly told his lawyers: "This bank wasn't in the business of making money. It was in the business of disbursing money." (*Insight*, March 11th, 1991) In his defence he said that the bank was an agent of Italian government policy. Sources close to him claimed: "BNL is not a bank. It is a source of Italian government funding."

BNL money was the lifeline of Iraqi efforts to become self-sufficient in the production of various armaments. Yet more than a half of billion dollars worth of credit that BNL Atlanta approved carry no names, so it is impossible to determine what they financed. However an Italian intelligence report of September 1989 from SISMI, the Italian intelligence service, to Prime Minister Giulio Andreotti, linked loans coming from this BNL branch to Iraq's Condor 2 missile program. This $1 billion project involved West Germany, Austria, and Brazil in developing an intermediate-range nuclear-capable missile. "It should be underlined that various domestic and foreign companies involved in the Condor 2 missile project have been helped thanks to the financial operations conducted by the BNL-Atlanta branch." (*Financial Times*, May 3rd, 1991)

Congressman Henry Gonzalez, a Democrat from Texas and Chairman of the House of Representatives' Committee on Banking, Finance and Urban Affairs, which investigated BNL, obtained a confidential memo showing that top ranking administration officials from a Cabinet-level department "had knowledge that BNL money was being used to purchase military goods."

"This administration official was concerned that the relation of BNL financing of military articles would be bad for his particular program because it would cause considerable adverse congressional reaction and press coverage," Gonzalez revealed. "He stated in the memo: In the worst-case scenario, investigators would find a direct link to the financing of Iraqi military expenditures, particularly the Condor missile." (*Village Voice*, March 12th, 1991)

The Department of Justice led the effort to block any investigation. While BNL Atlanta issued more than 2,500 letters of credit to Iraqi firms, only a handful of them have been disclosed. According to a report commissioned by the Simon Wiesenthal Center, a list has been compiled- but it is being kept secret by BNL, the Italian government, and by the U.S. Attorney General. None of these sources would release it to Gonzalez's Committee or the Italian Senate which conducted it's own investigation into the affair the Italian press dubbed: "Iraqgate."

The loans to Iraq were not reported to the U.S. Federal Reserve or the bank's headquarters in Rome. When Gonzalez asked Federal Reserve Chairman Alan Greenspan for information relating to a Bank of Italy audit of BNL, he was refused. Nor did the State Department or the Treasury Department turn over any records they had pertaining to the loans. (*The Nation*, May 13th, 1991)

Former Attorney General Dick Thornburgh was

equally uncooperative. On September 26th, 1990, he wrote to Gonzalez saying that he was disappointed in Gonzalez's decision to ignore the strong objections of the Department of Justice about the BNL matter. He told him: "This is a sensitive case with national security concerns" and that the Congressional investigation Gonzalez was heading would "significantly diminish the Department's ability to successfully prosecute this matter."

Gonzalez wrote back on September 28th, 1990 saying that he failed to see how "interviewing employees from the Federal Reserve Board, the Federal Reserve Bank of Atlanta, the Department of Banking and Finance of the State of Georgia, and current and former employees of BNL would significantly diminish the Justice Department's ability to successfully prosecute this matter."

On October 5th, 1990, Gonzalez received a letter from FBI Director William Sessions explaining to him how worried he was "over the possibility of grand jury information being inadvertently disclosed in Congressional proceedings and how the Committee's actions may prevent further cooperation by witnesses."

It's unfortunate that the heads of two of the leading judicial and law enforcement branches of the U.S. government have so little respect or confidence in Congress's ability to investigate a financial scandal. Also, if the Administration had no role in helping Saddam Hussein to acquire loans from BNL, what are the "national security concerns" Thornburgh was so worried about disclosing?

Could a tiny branch of an Italian bank give out more than $5 billion in loans to Iraq without any official in Washington discovering it?

"Even more sobering is the suggestion that someone in the administration did know and chose not to share this information with the Congress or the press," says Gonzalez.

Gonzalez finds it difficult to believe that the U.S. intelligence community or its allies abroad did not know about the application of technology being transferred to Iraq. Or that BNL escaped the attention of the intelligence community.

"These organizations monitor overseas telexes and phone conversations," he declared to Congress in February 1991. Did they fail to discover the over 3,000 telexes between BNL and Iraqi government agencies, many providing information detailing loans to companies that were building the Taji complex and other militia related projects with Iraq?

The Democrats on the Subcommittee concluded that the reason the Administration was supporting Iraq was due to an "inconsistent and unpredictable foreign policy." (*Washington Post*, June 24th, 1991)

They missed the point. Far from being a policy failure, the loans' goal was to arm Iraq and it was a resounding success. If it weren't for the information the Israelis provided to the FBI in Atlanta, neither the illegal use of BNL to fund the Iraqi military machine, nor the wider Iraqgate scandal, would ever have been made public.

Arming Iran: Israel and America's Big Secret

Arms sales play a big role in the covert Israeli-American relationship. To this day most Americans and Israelis believe that the only weapons the Americans sold to Iran were those which were part of the arms-for-hostages deals which became known as Irangate. All other arms sales were believed to have been carried out by "private dealers" not acting on any official government orders.

However like most arms sales, arms sales to Iran were completely sanctioned by both governments. Despite the policy of both governments to deny any connection to any arms dealer when he is arrested for selling arms to Iran, in most cases, if not all, this was a lie.

In fact, American and Israeli arms sales to Iran began even before the Reagan administration took office. They are part of the "October Surprise"

conspiracy which began to leak into the mainstream press in May of 1991 when Gary Sick
wrote an Op-Ed on the subject in the *New York
Times*.

It was easy for the White House to discredit
journalists from leftist and progressive magazines
who wrote about this conspiracy, but Sick was a
former member of the National Security Center
for Persian affairs in the Carter Administration
and an Adjunct Professor of Middle East Politics
at Columbia University. He was credible.

Sick had authored an earlier book about Iran
entitled *All Fall Down.* After he began conducting research for a book on the Iran Contra affair
and came across curious incidents and events
which could be neither explained nor ignored, he
concluded that before he could even begin to write
about Iran Contra, he had to first resolve this question of whether an "October Surprise" did or did
not occur.

Despite a Congressional whitewash in the fall
of 1992, I, along with many other investigative
journalists, believe that the Reagan campaign
team did make a deal with the Iranians to delay
the release of the U.S. hostages.

Sick's interpretation of the events begins
shortly after former CIA director William Casey
became Ronald Reagan's campaign manager in
February 1980. Until then Reagan's team was

confident that nothing could go wrong with the campaign, considering the political landscape and the sour state of the economy. Casey thought so too until a meeting at the Mayflower Hotel in Washington, when two Iranian brothers convinced him otherwise.

The Iranians were the Hashemi brothers, Cyrus and Jamshid. Cyrus was a former CIA operative turned arms dealer and Jamshid a successful businessman- both of them were well connected in the highest echelons of the Iranian revolutionary circles. The two of them urged Casey to do something to prevent Carter from garnering political capital from freeing the hostages before the elections. The seeds for an "October Surprise" were planted.

"Of all the people I talked to in the Reagan team it became clear that the one thing they were really worried about was the hostage issue," Sick told me during an interview in a West Side restaurant in mid-1992. "To some it became an obsession, that Carter would steal the election from them, take from them something which they felt rightfully belonged to them- the Presidency of the United States."

During the Republican convention in mid-July, the core group of those running the campaign met, and said, essentially, "look, we are down to the last run, we will win, but the hostages issue could be a problem." Just to be on the safe side, everyone would use their own channels and contacts to explore different possibilities.

At this point, Sick contends, at least three things happened: someone closely linked to this inner circle contacted Yasser Arafat's right hand man Bassam Abu Sharif. Sharif would later tell an American journalist that he remembered the name of the person he met to be O'Brian, and that he had boasted of his close ties with 'Ronnie', probably a reference to Ed Meese crony and co-conspirator Earl Brian.

Sharif was asked to put them in contact with the Iranians. In return the incoming Reagan Administration would formally recognize the PLO. This channel led nowhere as the PLO had lost many of their key contacts after the Iranian revolution.

A second effort was directed through former President Richard Nixon, who flew to London and met with Alan Bristow of Bristow Helicopters. Bristow had run the premier helicopter service to the Iranian oilfields up until the outbreak of the revolution. According to a September 1989 interview with Bristow in *The Sunday Telegraph*, Nixon's discussion centered on whether it was possible to put together an independent rescue operation. How many helicopters would be needed? What would the risks be? Nixon was exploring the possibility of a privately funded operation.

The third outcome was Casey's channel which originated via a series of meetings in Madrid in July 1980, set up by Cyrus Hashemi a few weeks after the Republican convention. He met with Mehdi Karrubi, the head of the Martyrs' Foundation, one of the most significant institutions of the revolution and now Speaker of the Iranian Parliament. Casey proposed that the Iranians hold off delivering the hostages until after the election. In return he would see to it that Reagan would return all of Iran's frozen assets and ensure a steady supply of military equipment and spare parts for Iran's armed forces, which since the days of the Shah had used only American-made weapons.

Several things happened: Iran began negotiating with the Carter administration through Sadegh Tabatabai, the brother-in-law of one of Khomeni's sons and one of Khomeni's closest advisors. When he requested arms for the release of the hostages, Carter turned him down, troubled by the moral implications of trading arms for hostages. What Carter didn't realize was that there was another offer on the table.

"Even today some of the people involved in those negotiations can't bring themselves to believe that the Iranians were negotiating with both sides," Sick contends.

Next came the mysterious rendezvous in early October 1980 at the L'Enfant Plaza Hotel in Washington, D.C. between an Iranian emissary (possibly Houshang Lavi, an American-Iranian arms dealer who maintained close contacts with the Mossad and could have been sent at Israel's behest) and Robert McFarlane, Richard Allen, and Reagan's campaign adviser Lawrence Silberman. Allen says he rebuffed any deal proposed at that meeting. McFarlane would later claim that he couldn't remember the identity of the "Iranian exile" he had met.

Then, on September 22nd, the Iran-Iraq war broke out.

"Let's assume you are a Republican and you think you have a deal with Karrubi and are now aware of negotiations with the Administration," Sick points out. "You think the Iranians are up to something. With the war under-way you must assume they are going to be very eager to gain arms quickly and thus Carter would be in an excellent position to make a deal and pull off an early hostage release. Carter wasn't pursuing it like that but Reagan's people believed he was and that's what's important."

The next crucial event happened between October 10th and 13th, when the Reagan campaign's foreign policy adviser, Richard Allen, learned through contacts in the CIA that Carter was planning a second rescue mission. The Administration was riddled with political enemies who relayed information to the Republicans because of anger at Carter over his handling of the hostage crisis and/or his attempts to scale-back the CIA. Allen was told that the White House was trying to determine the exact location at which the hostages were being held before sending the rescue team.

In fact, while Carter was involved in the negotiations he had no intention of launching a rescue mission which might risk the lives of the hostages. "It wasn't his style," says Sick. Although a second rescue mission was planned he was not planning to implement it except as a last resort. Allen didn't know that, and, even if he had known it, he probably wouldn't have believed it. From his perspective, it was now just a matter of time before a second rescue attempt would be made.

Former ambassador to Saudi Arabia, Morocco, and Afghanistan, Robert Neuman, remembers how worried Casey was about an "October Surprise" before the election. "He held daily meetings during the campaign to try and figure out what the Iranians might do," Neuman recounts.

Casey believed the uncertainty was too great for these crucial last few weeks of the campaign and that he had better re-establish contact with the Iranians. It was time to stop talking generalities and sweeten the pot.

The final details of a secret agreement would be worked out during a series of meetings in Paris between October 15th and 20th. The Iranians would agree to delay the release of the hostages in return for a commitment by the U.S. to supply Iran with more than $5 billion in arms to fight its war with Iraq.

In addition to the Iranian team, those attending the Paris meetings included Israeli representatives, Cyrus Hashemi, Casey, Allen, Bud McFarlane, and veteran CIA officer Donald Gregg. When Reagan took office Gregg became George Bush's top national security aide. Every researcher believes that it would have been inconceivable for George Bush not to have been there and that in fact he was seen on the tarmac in Paris by the pilot and CIA asset Gunther Russbacher.

It was at this stage that Israel took on a significant role in the affair.

Two former Israeli intelligence officials (other than Ari Ben Menashe) told Sick that officials with the Reagan campaign travelled to Israel after the first meetings in Madrid to ensure that Israel would agree to act as a conduit for the arms which Casey had promised.

Israel needed no prodding. It had a clear interest in a Reagan victory. It wanted to sell arms to Iran, for economic reasons, as well as to maintain their intelligence contacts and as a means to ensure the safety and emigration of Iranian Jews. Also, Prime Minister Menachem Begin and his Cabinet feared that Carter's second term would bring pressure on Israel to make concessions to expand the Camp David Accords, concessions which many believed would compromise Israel's security.

Israeli involvement in the affair deepened on September 28th when the first of two bizarre statements were made by the Israeli government. As reported by Israel Radio and BBC *Middle East Report*, Mordechai Zippori, then acting Minister of Defence, stated that "Israel could help Iran with weapons if they were to change their policies toward Israel." On October 18th the Associated Press quoted Zippori as repeating literally exactly the same statement.

"Read this as a signal that whoever was involved with the negotiations from the Iranian side wanted some type of acknowledgement from the top that Israel would supply the arms that were being discussed in the negotiations with Casey," comments Sick.

Another surprising statement came from Israel the following day when, in response to no question, Prime Minister Begin acknowledged for the first time ever that "Israel provided arms and instructors to train the Kurdish fighters in Northern

Iraq". The statement has never been repeated, nor denied.

"Begin's remark was a hint to the Iranians, essentially reminding them: look, we have helped you in the past against the Iraqis, if you're looking for help in your new battle with them, keep us in mind," Sick suggests.

Between October 21 and 23rd Israel sent a planeload of F-4 fighter aircraft tires to Iran, the first shipment of spare parts agreed under the new agreement.

Sick is the first one to admit he has no smoking gun and doubts if one even exists in the way of any extensive written documentation. Experienced intelligence officers were employed to clean up any damaging evidence such as entries in hotel registers, flight records etc.

"It was a professional covert operation," he says. "Historical events of this nature are rarely documented."

There is evidence however that the French intelligence service was involved in the operation and actually set up the meetings. Sick has talked to people who say they have seen French intelligence reports on the affair. Also, secondary people involved might have kept personal written records, if for no other reason other than to protect themselves.

If documentation does exist which details the

quantities and types of weapons the U.S. and Israel supplied to Iran, it may very well be the same secret agreement Amiram Nir, Prime Minister Peres advisor on terrorism and one of Israel's main link in the Iran Contra affair, was referring to when he met the *Washington Post*'s Bob Woodward in London in June 1988. Nir revealed that the agreement led to a number of covert actions which all had "common tactical elements" and were "initialled by both heads of state."

After Sick's book came out a number of mainstream publications published articles "proving" that there was no "October Surprise". Since some of the sources Sick used were either arms dealers or intelligence officials, they were deemed not credible and therefore, according to those news stories, there was no "October Surprise".

It's as if the mainstream press had said "Bush, Meese, and Allen would never lie to the American people," and "of course there were no secret dealings or corruption in the Reagan White House."

The extremely quick dismissal by *Newsweek* and *The New Republic* of the "October Surprise" story hasn't fooled anyone (except the majority of the American people).

In response to claims that Sick and others use "less than credible sources" one simply asks not whether a source is an honest, incorruptible man but rather whether his information checks out. The problem is that powerful people, like Edwin Meese, Richard Allen, George Bush and Robert MacFarlane, despite their publicly acknowledged role in covert or even illegal activities, are never called liars or frauds by these same publications who dismiss smaller operators in the same field. Anyone who claims that "the Reagan people would never commit such a treasonous act" have never studied what those same people did once they got into the White House.

As often happens when mainstream journalists are eager to throw the "crazy conspiracy theory" label at independent investigators, the two main questions were never addressed. Despite the many attempts to interfere, are we to assume that the Reagan campaign kept a safe distance from any of Carter's efforts to have the hostages released? Was it merely a coincidence that the hostages were released on the day of Reagan's inauguration or that Donald Gregg, a member of the National Security Council under Carter, was appointed National Security Adviser to Vice President Bush (the only National Security Advisor to a Vice President ever appointed)?

Still, there are a number of mysteries surrounding the "October Surprise" that still don't make sense. Let's assume there was a prearranged deal. The Iranians hated Carter because he'd refused to extradite the Shah, they didn't want him to win the election.

They made a deal with Reagan's campaign team not to release the hostages until after the election. Why then did they wait until the third week of January to release them? What did they have to gain by holding on to them after the election? If the Reagan campaign team did make a deal, didn't they realize that having the hostages released at literally the same moment as Reagan was being inaugurated would look just a bit too coincidental? Having them released in mid-November would certainly have made it look like the Iranians had done Carter in.

If Reagan's team did make a deal, what kept them to the deal? Once the hostages were released, the Iranians had nothing to bargain with. Once Reagan was in office, any deals concluded before the election could be cancelled unless the Administration simply wanted to keep its word and live up to its side of the bargain.

In fact, that is exactly what happened. The Administration permitted Israel to sell U.S. made arms to Iran as part of the "October Surprise" arrangement until the end of 1982. Avraham Tamir, former Director General of Israel's Foreign Ministry, claims that by December 1982 the permission the U.S. had granted Israel ended. It was at this time that the U.S. began to support Iraq in the Iran-Iraq war, so it would be logical that they would want Israel to stop selling arms to Iran.

It must have taken the Iranians a while to figure out what to do. But it was really quite simple. They had taken hostages before and the Americans sold them arms. So in March 1984 they kidnap CIA station chief of Beirut William Buckley and other Americans. The story repeats itself: the Iranians want arms; the Americans want their hostages back. The only difference was that by this time there was no presidential election to manipulate.

During the Congressional investigation into the "October Surprise" Indiana Democratic Congressman Lee Hamilton asked Yitzhak Rabin to allow twenty Israelis to testify before a Congressional investigation of the so-called "October Surprise". These Israelis were suspected of aiding the Reagan campaign team in 1980 in delaying the release of the U.S. hostages held in Iran. (*Inside Israel*, April 1993)

Rabin, never losing an opportunity to help his old friend George Bush and the Republican party, initially refused, but agreed to appoint 70 year old Reserve General Rafael Vardi to lead an Israeli investigation of the allegations. Amongst those questioned by Vardi were former Defence Ministers Ariel Sharon and Moshe Arens, former Mossad chief Yitzhak Hofi, former Director Gen-

erals of the Foreign Ministry David Kimche and
Avraham Tamir, and arms dealers Al Schwimmer
and Yaakov Nimrodi. His report concluded that
"the allegations were baseless."

One of those questioned claims an affidavit
disputing the charges was put in front of him and
he was told to sign it. He refused.

It is important to remember who Vardi was. In
1987 American officials had also wanted to investigate Israelis believed to be involved in the Iran
Contra scandal. Instead of allowing the principals
to testify in Washington, the Israeli government
appointed him to produce a chronology of events
for the U.S. Congress. Then, as in the case of his
latest report, the Israeli role was minimized.

Critics of the "October Surprise" report point
out that Vardi's investigation was conducted with
unseeming haste and that no non-Israelis who
could verify the allegations were questioned.

As a reward for a job well done, Vardi was
shortly after appointed Rabin's Chief Adviser on
Intelligence to deal with "special projects." Most
of the security establishment, including the
Shabak (General Security Services) and Mossad,
was against the political appointment, claiming
that Vardi had no experience in the intelligence
field. They worried that because of a blatant political appointment, the Prime Minister would lack
an advisor on all matters relating to intelligence.

U.S. Arms Sales
to Iran After 1980

What is important is what the Reagan and Bush Administrations did AFTER the 1980 Presidential election.

If the "October Surprise" theory is eventually proven correct, and the arms sales by Israel to Iran on behalf of the U.S. are verified, then the next question to be asked is what happened after December 1982.

According to Avraham Tamir, then director general of Israel's foreign ministry, the permission given by the Americans until then for Israel to sell U.S. made weapons to Iran was withdrawn. (Interview with Avraham Tamir by the author, Tel Aviv, January 1992)

It's likely that if a deal was made in 1980 to ensure a steady supply of U.S. arms to be delivered by way of Israel, by the end of 1982 someone in the White House must have figured out that there was no reason for Israel to make middleman money selling American arms to Iran. The American government could do it, covertly, and at the same time earn money for covert operations, or as William Casey liked to refer to them, "off-the-shelf" operations.

Did America sell arms to Iran between 1981 and 1985? This question is paramount to determining whether Operation Staunch and the official policy of the White House was nothing but a deception that the American public bought hook, line and sinker.

Operation Demevand

Although it never made its way into the mainstream press, the alternative press, *The Nation*, *The Village Voice*, *The Progressive*, and *In These Times*, have given extensive coverage to Operation Demevand.

Named for a mountain range in Iran, this was a White House operation to sell massive amounts of arms to Iran, covertly and illegally.

Barbara Honneger, in her book *October Surprise*, gave one of the earliest reports on massive arms sales from the U.S. to Iran (pp. 179-183). Although many of the sources remained anonymous, she has to be given a lot of credit for investigating a secret agenda that up until then had gone virtually undetected. Her sources told her that arms shipments began in 1981, and by 1986 more than $15 billion worth of arms had been redirected to Iran. She quotes Richard Muller, a former colonel in the Marine reserves, as claiming that secret NATO military supplies stored in reforger stores throughout Europe were being drawn-down and sold to Iran, as well as to rebel forces the administration was supporting in Angola, Afghanistan and Central America. The proceeds went to the Pentagon's "black budget" for covert activities.

There was one aspect of the operation that Honneger couldn't figure out. Why would the U.S. knowingly leave itself unable to defend against a conventional attack from Warsaw Pact countries? The rationale for the reforger stores was to give NATO additional time before a decision to use nuclear weapons had to be made.

One of her sources, a former CIA official stationed in Germany for a number of years, finally answered that question for her. That was exactly the intention, to deplete the reforger stores in order to force NATO commanders to go nuclear. If the Soviets knew of this likelihood, it would serve to counter their more than two-to-one superiority in conventional forces. Thus the threat of using nuclear weapons, the source claimed, brought the Soviets to the Intermediate Nuclear Forces bargaining table.

The U.S.'s allies would obviously refuse to go along with such a plan, but they didn't know because they were given falsified lists of the inventory of the supply depots.

The source revealed that the Soviet were "told" about the operation when in 1986 the U.S. traded an Eastern Bloc spy named Koecher, for Natan

Sharansky. Koecher told his KGB bosses in Prague about the draw-down at the NATO stores.

Honneger's initial reports of official U.S. government complicity in arms sales to Iran were verified by other investigative journalists. ABC News European correspondent Pierre Salinger quoted Swedish arms dealer Sven Klang as saying that he was involved in arms shipments initiated by the Reagan-Bush Administration in 1981 to deliver F-4 fighter jet engines to Iran from NATO warehouses through the Belgium-based ASCO company.

A *Newsday* reporter discovered that in 1981 customs agents at the U.S. embassy in London told State Department officials that two Iranian-born arms dealers were shipping U.S. military equipment to Iran. The Customs agents were ordered by the State Department officials to drop their investigation. The newspaper also reported that British merchant marine captain Thomas Screech ran ships carrying 2,000 U.S. aerial bomb fuses from Portugal to Bandar Abbas, Iran, in the summer 1982, with cargo which originated in U.S. government ammunition plants. When Screech reported these deliveries to the U.S. embassy in London, the State Department told them to ignore him. (Honneger, pp. 195-196)

Operatives from one "Demevand operation" operating out of the U.S. Embassy in Paris claimed that profits of $400 million from these arms sales were used to supply weapons to U.S.-supported rebel groups in Nicaragua, Afghanistan, Angola and Ethiopia.

Details of this arms pipeline were discovered in August 1985 when Lt. William Gillespie, 46, a missile expert, graduate of West Point, and veteran of two tours in Viet Nam, was caught in a sting operation in Orlando, Florida. (*Los Angeles Times*, August 2, 1985) From 1982 Gillespie worked on military projects with U.S.'s NATO allies at the army material command in Alexandria, Virginia.

The group operated through European Defence Associates (believed to be tied to a group of Israeli arms dealers), a company set up by Colonel Ralph Borman, then chief of the Pentagon's Office of Defence Cooperation in Paris and entrusted with monitoring international shipment of arms to Iran under Operation Staunch. In one sale European Defence Associates was involved in, more than a billion dollars worth of U.S. made weapons including tanks, missiles, submarines, and fighter jets, were to be transferred from U.S. stockpiles in Europe to arms caches in Iran.

Along with Paul Cutter, who worked for the U.S. Information Agency in the Soviet Union through the mid-1960s and spent five years in prison from 1976 to 1981 for importing rifles into

Yugoslavia, Gillespie and three other operatives were arrested by undercover Customs Agents when they tried to sell the agent more than $40 million in arms. Among the weapons included in the offer were Sidewinder, Sparrow, Harpoon, Phoenix, and French-made Exocet missiles. William Mott IV, officer at US embassy in London and founder of Spearhead Atlantic, did business with European Defence Associates and worked with Gillespie and Cutter. (Honneger, pp. 201-202)

Cutter originally kept quiet when sent to jail in 1985. He then discovered that Gillespie and the others didn't share the same fate. Found innocent after their testimony that Cutter was a government agent, it was believed that they were acting with government sanction. Cutter concluded he was set up and began talking to the press, claiming: "We all worked under the umbrella of U.S. Defence Department approval." (*New York Times*, December 5th, 1986)

He said his operation alone shifted at least $1.2 billion worth of military equipment to Iran from NATO supply depots in Europe.

Italy was another major trans-shipment point for U.S. arms to Iran. In November 1986, Italian Prime Minister Bennito Craxi ordered an inquiry into reports that small Italian ports of Tuscany and Talamore were being used for arms shipments to

Iran without the knowledge of the Italian government.

Official Statements from the Prime Ministers' office and Defence Minister Giovanne Spadolini said that there had not even been a tacit accord with the U.S. government on these shipments. Opposition legislators claimed that by October 1986 sixty ships full of arms had left the Italian port of Talamore. (*New York Times*, November 12th, 1986)

As the Italian government had no record of these shipments, they were believed to have been taken out of the military supplies kept by the U.S. army in Italy and sold covertly.

The Italian judge Carlo Palermo eventually wrote a 6,000 page report revealing that the CIA headquarters and U.S. Embassy in Rome, U.S. military bases in Italy and U.S. Naval Forces based on Maddelena near Sardinia, were all involved in the shipments of arms.

Paying the Price for Ollie North

Further evidence of pre-1985 U.S. arms sales to Iran can be found in Arif Durrani's testimony that he witnessed massive sales of U.S. arms between NATO supply depots and Iran. Although Oliver

North didn't go to jail, some people did for doing exactly what North told them to do. One of them is Arif Durrani.

I first heard about Durrani from Larry Lifschultz in March 1991. Lifschultz was a former South Asia correspondent of the *Far Eastern Economic Review* and believed Durrani was wrongfully convicted.

Lifschultz's investigation lasted more than a year and in the end he believed he had unlocked the details of an illicit world of arms trading linked to the Iran-Contra scandal. It was a side to the story that has never been told and one which has Israeli arms sales to Iran written all over it. If more widely known, many other aspects of Israel's role in Iran-Contra would become a lot clearer.

Durrani testified that he discovered the scope and volume of arms illegally shipped to Iran from NATO stores and NATO suppliers was hundreds of times greater than the size of shipments revealed at the Iran-Contra hearings. Durrani's own operation exported more than $750 million worth of arms to Iran. (*The Pamphleteer's Press*, East Haven, Connecticut, September 1991)

Durrani's story begins in the spring of 1986 when he was asked by the Israeli purchasing office in New York to meet with Manuel Jose Pires, a Portuguese arms merchant. Pires was working with Israel to locate more than 240 different parts which the Iranians were desperate for. Through Pires Durrani met senior officials of the U.S. government, including Oliver North. In September 1986 Durrani was asked by Pires to come to London to discuss future arms shipments with Oliver North at the Hilton Hotel. North told them that although the parts were ready for shipment, there would be a problem with export licenses. He said:

"You don't need them. It's all going to be authorized." (*Pamphlet*, p.12)

On October 2nd, 1986, Durrani arranged a shipment of the HAWK parts to Belgium and falsely signed a declaration that he had all the required export licenses. The next day he was arrested by U.S. Customs agents in Danbury, Connecticut, just weeks before the Iran Contra scandal broke. During his trial in the spring of 1987 CIA and NSC officials came to Bridgeport, Connecticut and denied under oath that Durrani was connected in any way to any U.S. government operation. The jury believed them and in mid-April 1987 sentenced the 41 year old Pakistani national to ten years in prison and a $2 million fine.

The judge did not allow Durrani's lawyers to introduce as evidence any parts of the Tower Commission Report which indicated that North was seeking HAWK parts which couldn't be procured within existing Israeli or American government inventories. Nor did he allow any classified government documents which might have supported Durrani's case. In sentencing him, Judge T. Gilroy Daly said that Durrani's "behavior might under other circumstances be considered by some as 'bordering on treason.'"

Lifschultz and his team realized that Pires was the key to proving Durrani's innocence. Looking into his past they discovered that he was a major player in Spanish arms sales to Iran using end-user certificates issued by the Brazilian Defence Ministry. (*El Tiempo*, December, 26th, 1988) He also specialized in selling arms to embargoed countries such as South Africa.

They also discovered that Pires met with Assistant U.S. Attorney Holly Fitzsimmons and U.S. Customs Agents in February 1987. While he was never indicted, records existed of communications between him and Durrani which showed that Pires had no connection with the U.S. government.

In Brussels, Lifschultz obtained a four hundred page report of a Belgian special police investigation showing how Brussels had been used by black market arms traffickers. Brussels was Pires' main shipment point. One of these deals was for 10,000 TOW missiles to Iran, via Israel in 1985.

Procuring 10,000 TOW missiles covertly is not an easy task. Only the U.S. and NATO's European inventories had such stocks available. The official Iran Contra story tells of TOW missiles being sold to Iran from stocks in the U.S. and Israel. Although no mention is made of them originating in NATO stocks, it's possible that this is exactly where they came from.

Ken Timmerman, an expert in the international arms trade, reported in 1987 that a major smuggling operation involving TOW missiles from NATO stockpiles in the U.S. and Europe was carried on inside the sealed customs zone of Brussels Zaventem International Airport. He quotes intelligence sources in France and West Germany as saying that General Bernard Rogers, then NATO's Commander in Chief and head of the U.S.-European command, ordered an internal investigation in 1986 of reports that TOW missiles from NATO warehouses in West Germany were diverted to Iran in 1985.

He further quotes a spokesperson for the Supreme Headquarters-Allied Powers in Europe in Belgium as saying that the investigation was "a political issue" and that "the Pentagon has ordered us not to comment on it." The intelligence official said General Rogers was "furious to learn that NATO weapons were being sold to Iran without his knowledge." (*The Nation*, July 18th-25th, 1987)

Timmerman cites Belgian customs documents showing that "at least 3,000 TOW missiles" were involved in a shell-game assembly operation. Chartered cargo planes arriving from military bases in the U.S. brought in the TOW warheads. Shortly after they taxied to a stop in the customs area, additional planes, carrying missile fuselages and motors from NATO storehouses in Bavaria, would pull up alongside them.

Since the warheads were never offloaded- and thus technically not imported into Belgium- no customs documents were required. The Belgian daily *Le Soir*, which surveyed the customs documents, concluded that the operation "had the benediction of the Pentagon." (*The Nation*, July 18-25th 1987)

Like most other investigative journalists writing about illegal U.S. arms sales to Iran and lacking top secret documents, Lifschultz relied heavily on the "two plus two" theory. Before the Tower Commission, former National Security Advisor Robert McFarlane testified that he and David Kimche, Israel's Director General of the Foreign Ministry, discussed the request by Israel for the U.S. to replace at least 500 TOW missiles to replenish Israeli stocks.

In the Belgian police file, Lifschultz noted an August 1st, 1985 sales contract between Kennard International of Panama and a Greek firm, for the sale of 5,000 TOW missiles. The police investigators explained to Lifschultz that they believe

Kennard International was a front company for the Israeli government to mask the sale of TOW missiles to the Greek firm which transferred the possession of the TOWs to Pires in Lisbon before they were shipped to Iran. The whole exercise was undertaken to hide the actual origins of the supplier.

This means that the number of missiles Israel shipped to Iran, as part of Israel's official story, i.e., the Shimon Peres-Yaakov Nimrodi-Al Schwimmer pipeline at the end of August and early September 1985, was 5,000, not 500 as the official version of events indicates.

One source Lifschultz calls "Max" claimed to have personal knowledge of the sales. In an interview in Brussels on March 23rd, 1990, Max described for him North's travels in Europe during September and October 1986. During that period a close associate in his firm personally observed Pires and North together, and said that during 1986 North was telling everybody, "You are working for the U.S. government. You are working for the Boss. Don't worry. You will have no problems. "

Willy de Greef, who directed Pires's office in Brussels for three years, told Lifschultz that Manuel Pires told him he had met Oliver North in London twice and that they fixed everything for the TOW shipment to Iran. The Belgian police file revealed how in 1985 Pires used military bases in Addis Ababa, Ethiopia, to fly TOW missiles from Israel and Europe to Bandar Abbas in Iran. Pires used TransEuropean Airways, an airline owned by George Mittleman, an Orthodox Jew in Belgium who earned his bread and butter flying Islamic pilgrimages to Mecca. It was the same charter airline that was used to fly Jews out of Ethiopia during Operation Moses in 1984. "The same planes which brought arms to Ethiopia en route to Iran, left carrying Jews destined for Israel," Durrani claims.

Why did the U.S. government not bother to indict or further investigate Pires as a co-conspirator in the Durrani case? Lifschultz speculates that Pires "knows too much" and has a long history of clandestine associations which Israel which some Western governments could not afford to have aired in an open courtroom.

Three weeks after Durrani was sentenced, on July 9th, 1987, Pires visited Durrani at the Federal Correctional Institution in Phoenix, Arizona. Pires indicated to Durrani that their conversation was being recorded. Pires tried to get Durrani to talk about various aspects of their transactions. After Durrani accused Pires of not coming to his aid, Pires replied it was a mistake and that he never imagined he would be given a ten year sentence. "It wasn't supposed to have happened that way," Pires said.

Durrani's lawyer, William Bloss can't understand how Pires was able to receive permission to see Durrani as he is not a family member and as it is customary for such visits to be proceeded by extensive background checks. He says: "There is no chance that a foreign national would just show up at a federal prison saying "I want to see my friend" and the warden would say 'Fine...just go on in.' It is impossible."

Durrani was told by personnel at the prison that the Pires visit was arranged at the request of a lawyer, "the woman from Connecticut."

Wasn't Pires concerned that he would be arrested if he travelled to the U.S.? Bloss speculates that a deal had been worked out giving him immunity from prosecution. Lifschultz spoke with a prison official who told him Pires met a U.S. Customs Agent and Assistant U.S. Attorney Holly Fitzsimmon in Phoenix and that Pires was working with the U.S. government on "matters which are classified."

In fact, Fitzsimmons did admit that she met Pires in Phoenix, but not that she arranged for him to visit Durrani. In an interview with Lifschultz, Fitsimmons claimed it was not a coincidence that Pires, the Customs Agent Steven Arruda, and herself were in Phoenix all at the same time. However since Pires had been a federal witness prior to the trial, she could not comment "as a matter of policy", nor would she admit that the U.S. Customs Office had arranged for Pires to see Durrani.

Lifschultz later discovered that Pires's visit was linked to a continuing U.S. Customs investigation about HAWK missile parts which agents believed Durrani had hidden at a secret location in the United States. Pires was in Phoenix as an informant for this investigation.

The customs office tried to get Durrani to tell Pires where these parts were hidden. "At the very least this means that the U.S. government was cooperating with Pires, for how long we don't know," Lifschultz concludes.

In a telephone interview in October 1990 Pires said that he had visited Durrani "officially... through legal channels", claiming Durrani owed him money from previous shipments. He denied meeting Fitzsimmons' U.S. Customs agents. When Lifschultz told Pires that Fitzsimmons had admitted to meeting Pires in Phoenix, Pires changed his story and claimed that they had only spoken by telephone.

Considering Oliver North only had to pay a fine of $150,000 and was sentenced to two years probation and 1,200 hours in community service at a drug program, Durrani got an unusually harsh sentence. The larger questions are whether arms sales to Iran were hundreds of times greater than the public has been told and whether or not the Pentagon knew about and collaborated in the transfer of weapons from NATO supply depots to Iran.

If this is the case, profits in the hundreds of millions of dollars were generated. How many covert operations they funded is anyone's guess.

Post Iran-Contra
U.S. Arms Sales to Iran

Another side of the Iran-Contra affair which has never become part of the official record took place in July 1987 meeting between then deputy CIA director Robert Gates and Iranian Defence Minister Mohamed Hosein Jalali at the Vista Hotel in Kansas City, Missouri. The meeting was to consummate an enormous weapons sale. The deal was to be a "pass through," meaning that the weapons would originate in U.S. or that Washington would replace Israeli stocks of any weapons sold from its stockpile. In other words, even after the Iran Contra scandal was made public, both Israel and the U.S. were still selling arms to Iran.

On February 23rd, 1987 the U.S. Customs branch at the U.S. Embassy in Rome cabled Washington that it had learned of an Israeli effort to ship TOW missiles to Iran. The report said that "a foreign national is attempting to acquire in Italy an end-user certïficate for the purchase of 10,000 TOW missiles." The sale was to have taken place in Switzerland.

In that transaction Israel sold Iran a total of 12,000 US-made TOW missiles in three batches of 4,000 each. On November 8th, 1987, the *International Herald Tribune* reported that "Israel might have negotiated to sell up to $750 million in arms to Iran late last summer." The package was said to include U.S. made TOW anti-tank missiles, Israeli made Gabriel air-to-surface missiles, F-4 and F-5 aircraft engine parts, tanks and jeeps. The sale, the paper reported, was executed through a third party based in Geneva, Switzerland.

During that summer, the Israelis held three meetings in Geneva with an Iranian delegation headed by Khomeini's son Ahmed and which also included Parliament chairman Hashemi Rafsanjani. (*La Suisse*, August 14th, 1987)

The two day meeting was held without the knowledge of Iran's ambassador to the UN or that of the local Counsel-General. The Iranians sent a cabinet-level committee to continue contacts with the Israelis and the Americans. (*Middle East Insider*, August 17th, 1987)

The two sides also discussed a plan for increasing Jewish emigration from Iran in return for Israeli arms. More than 25,000 Jews were to leave Iran over the next six months. (*London Observer*, September 13th, 1987)

An exodus of Iranian Jews followed. On September 15th, the *Turkish Daily News* of Ankara reported that more than 30,000 Jews would be allowed to leave Iran via Turkey in the following month and that Iran's Ambassador to Turkey, Manushehr Mottaki, had been involved in the negotiations. Austrian Foreign Minister Alois Mock, confirmed in the report that 30,000 Jews from Iran left for Israel, via buses to Pakistan, to go on from there by air to Austria and Tel Aviv. Mock told reporters in New York on October 3rd, 1987, that 5,100 Iranians Jews had come through Austria since 1983, of which, 1,483 arrived in the first eight months of 1987.

It is very unlikely that Israel would have been able to sell that amount of U.S. made TOW missiles without the White House's full acknowledgement, perhaps even without acting on behalf of Washington.

The Asian Iran Contra Affair

Larry Lifschultz, the investigative journalist who has closely followed Arif Durrani's case, also found Ben Menashe to be a very credible source on another little-known aspect of the Iran Contra affair.

Lifschultz discovered how in the mid-1980s Pakistan became a conduit for the sale of hundreds of millions of dollars worth of U.S. made arms to Iran and how the $2 billion supply line which was established by the White House to provide arms to the rebels in Afghanistan, was exploited as a source of weapons for the Nicaraguan Contras and to fund covert operations. (*Far Eastern Economic Review*, December 1991)

Ben Menashe says that for more than three years an Israeli military logistics and advisory team was based in Pakistan and managed the secret arms pipeline to Iran. Lifschultz confirmed this story with two Pakistani intelligence sources who were involved in the operation and another who worked for the National Logistics Cell, a special agency under the command of the Pakistani army which served as the main carrier of the weapons to Iran. Another source, a prominent figure in Pakistan's Shia community with close connections to Pakistan's Inter-Services Intelligence (ISI), also confirmed the allegation.

A former Pakistani intelligence agent described the network as one of Islambad's "biggest secrets," (*The New Delhi Times*, November 24th, 1991)

One diversion involved $300 million worth of weapons. Although sent to Pakistan and paid for by Congress, who thought the weapons were going to the Afghan rebels, the arms were re-routed, and after arriving in Peshawar, where paperwork showed them to have arrived at their intended destination, they were sent on to Iran. The Iranian government paid $300 million cash for these weapons, the amount being deposited into a bank account in Luxembourg.

"This was the first major attempt to create additional funding for those people in the American intelligence community linked to the Contras," Ben Menashe told Lifschultz.

This illegal diversion of U.S. government funds was not the first or the last. In 1987 allegations were made by the Federation for American-Afghan Action that only $390 million of the $1.09 billion of aid approved by Congress between 1980 and 1986 to support the Mujahideen rebels had actually reached them. The chairman of the group, Andrew Evia, said that between 1980 and 1984 of the $342 million appropriated by Congress, only $36 million of military aid arrived in Afghanistan. Evia believes that overall

70% of the assistance never even reached the rebel groups.

Yet it isn't even certain that the money was diverted to support the Contras in Central America.

It's possible that somebody wanted the money to go to the Nicaraguan Contras, but Contra leaders say even Ollie North's money didn't reach them. The question is, where did the money go? Where did $700 million go and was this operation a joint Israeli -American effort?

Did Israel Help Expose the White House's Involvement in the Pan-Am 103 Crash?

If the entire story behind the bombing of Pan-Am 103 over Lockerbie, Scotland, in December 1988 is ever fully exposed, most people just simply will not believe it. Not only were various agencies of the U.S. government at least partially responsible for the terrorist attack, the Bush Administration tried to cover-up their own involvement. However what has yet to be exposed is the role the Israeli government played in exposing the White House role in the scandal.

It is important to understand that as soon as Bush took office in January 1989, U.S.-Israeli relations took a nosedive. Bush disliked Israel not for any of the conventional reasons often put forward, (eg., he was anti-Semitic, pro-Arab, had ties to the oil industry) but rather because Israel-supporters in Congress got in the way of the White House's secret agendas. After Bush was elected, he and Baker sat down and discussed revenge.

Most importantly, Israel interfered with the ability to sell arms to Arabs, particularly Saudis, who pay for their weapons in cash. For instance, in February 1986 the Administration had to postpone indefinitely a proposed $1.9 billion arms sale of anti-aircraft missiles and advanced jet fighters intended for Jordan. AIPAC and pro-Israel supporters in Congress led a massive resistance to the sale. As a result, the White House delayed a $1 billion arms package for Saudi Arabia.

When he became President, Bush was not going to let AIPAC repeat those victories. His administration was going to sell arms to whomever it found profitable. Rather than allow Israel and AIPAC to get in the way of White House policy, Bush merely took American Middle East foreign policy underground. Like so many of Bush's policies, it became a covert operation.

So when Pan-Am 103 was blown up, the events surrounding the disaster had to be covered-up or a number of other covert operations run by the White House would have been exposed.

It was no coincidence that an Israeli-born private investigator living in New York was the first to blow the real story behind the bombing of Pan-

Am 103 open, despite U.S. government attempts to cover it up. If the true story behind Pan-Am 103 ever finally does come out, Yuval Aviv and the Israeli government will be able to take much of the credit.

I met a lot of strange characters while conducting research for this book, but Yuval Aviv was by far the oddest. I met Aviv for the first time in October 1991. After a three hour meeting I walked out of his Madison Avenue office with my mind boggling. Aviv has a certain charm about him that makes him very likable, even if you don't quite trust his information or understand his motives. He claims to be a former Mossad officer who immigrated to the U.S. in 1978. Shortly after, he opened his own investigating firm called Interfor.

Aviv told me alot of stories, some of which I checked out and found to be false. Some were verified by other sources. Like most sources investigative journalists come across, some of Aviv's information was good, some wasn't. Where Aviv does come through with flying colors though is in his version of what happened to Pan-Am 103, the plane that blew up over Lockerbie, Scotland on December 21st 1988. Without Aviv's contacts in Israel, it is doubtful that the true story behind the bombing would ever have come out. The Shamir government's desire to "stick it to Bush" played a key role in aiding Aviv's investigation.

Aviv's firm was hired by Pan-Am's insurer in the spring of 1989 to investigate the crash. Of all the journalists and intelligence sources I met who knew Aviv, all of them agreed that his report on Pan-Am 103 is the closest thing yet to the truth. The only problem is that what he has to say about the incident isn't what the Bush Administration wants to hear. In September 1989, Interfor's report was made public. In it, Aviv claimed that a CIA team headquartered in Western Germany is largely responsible for the bombing.

That's not what the U.S. Administration claims. For the first two years after the crash all the evidence pointed to Syria and Iran as the culprits. It was believed that Iran bankrolled the operation in retaliation for the July 3rd, 1988 shooting down by the USS Vincennes of an Iranian plane, killing 290 people in the Persian Gulf. Previously U.S. investigators had traced a wire transfer of several million dollars from Teheran to a bank account in Vienna controlled by the Popular Front for the Liberation of Palestine, specifically the General Command under the leadership of Ahmad Jibril. (*US News And World Report*, November 25th, 1991)

Outbreak of the Gulf War changed all that. When Saddam's troops rolled into Kuwait, the Administration needed to bring Syria into the coalition effort. The following summer Bush sat down with Assad in Geneva and ushered in a new era in Syrian-American relations. As a result, focus had to be deflected from Syrian-sponsored Ahmad Jibril's terrorist group.

Lo and behold, in November 1991 U.S. prosecutors announced that their three year investigation produced no evidence that either Iran or Syria were involved. Instead, they believed two Libyan intelligence officials and government in Tripoli were responsible for the bombing. (*New York Times*, November 15th, 1991)

President Bush would publicly remark: "The Syrians took a bum rap on this." (*Time*, April 27th, 1992)

The U.S. government based its case on a tiny piece of plastic embedded in a shirt that came from the suitcase which held the bomb. Miraculously, it survived two harsh Scottish winters. A British forensic expert compared it to the fragment of a bomb-timer used to destroy a French DC-10 jet that exploded over Africa nine months after the Lockerbie tragedy, and found them to be identical. Based on this evidence indictments were issued for the two Libyan intelligence officials. (It seems the Justice Department felt they'd look a little silly asking Muammar Khaddafi to turn himself in to the American authorities.)

American and British investigators speculate that Iran and Libya were plotting simultaneously to blow up an American jet, but that the Libyans succeeded first. Khaddafi, it was claimed, wanted revenge for the 1986 bombing of Tripoli and Benghazi by U.S. warplanes. (Why did he wait more than two and a half years to get it?). They say the bomb was first loaded as unaccompanied luggage on an Air-Malta flight which departed Lauq Airport in Malta and connected with the Pan-Am flight in Frankfurt. Why a terrorist would take such an indirect route and risk detection was left unexplained.

The official U.S. government's version of events is quite different from Aviv's. The former Israeli intelligence official explains that his investigation revealed the origin of the terrorist attack to have been a rogue CIA group providing protection to a Syrian drug operation which transported drugs from the Middle East to the U.S. via Frankfurt. Aviv says the CIA did nothing to break up the drug operation because the traffickers were also helping them send weapons to Iran to facilitate the hostage release and for the Nicaraguan Contras.

Part of Aviv's assertions were backed-up by *NBC News* a year later when they reported on October 30th, 1990 that the Drug Enforcement Administration (DEA) was investigating a Middle East based heroin operation to determine whether it was used by terrorists to place a bomb on Pan-

Am 103. NBC said that Pan-Am flights out of Frankfurt had been used by the DEA to fly informants and heroin into Detroit as part of its sting operation. It claimed the terrorists might have discovered what the DEA was doing and switched one of their bags with one containing the bomb. The DEA denied any connection to the undercover operation. (*Barron's*, December 17th, 1990)

Aviv explains that the method of drug smuggling was quite simple. One person would check a piece of luggage onto the plane and an accomplice working in the baggage department would switch it with an identical piece containing the narcotics. He says that that fatal night, a Syrian terrorist organization aware of how the drug operation worked slipped a bomb inside the suitcase going on the plane. Aviv asserts that Monzer Al-Kassar, a Syrian drugs and arms smuggler previously mentioned, set the drug smuggling operation up through Frankfurt in 1987. The CIA, the DEA, and the West German secret police, the BKA, observed its activities, but didn't interfere in order to acquire information. Al-Kassar is well connected. The head of Syrian intelligence, Ali Issa Duba, is his brother-in-law, and his wife is a member of Syrian President Hafez Assad's family.

This was the same Monzer Al-Kassar who helped Oliver North supply Polish-made weapons to the Nicaraguan Contras in 1985 and 1986. Along with his three brothers Al-Kassar had built a multi-million dollar empire on military deals in Eastern and Western Europe. Administration officials who discussed these deal said Al-Kassar had clear business links with the Abu Nidal terrorist organization. (*Los Angeles Times*, July 17, 1987)

The officials said that Al-Kasser maintained offices in Warsaw and was a major broker for the Polish-owned weapons company Cenzin. The first arms purchase by North from Al-Kassar totalling $1 million was sent by boat to an unidentified Caribbean port in the fall of 1985 and was later distributed to the Contra fighters. In April of that year a second shipment of Polish arms was sold to the CIA as part of this transaction. (*Los Angeles Times*, July 17th, 1987)

In another part of the deal, more than $42 million were laundered through BCCI bank accounts in the Cayman Islands. Al-Kassar earned more than $1 million. (*Private Eye*, October 25th, 1991)

Aviv wrote in his report that a special hostage rescue team was on the doomed aircraft led by Army Major Charles McKee, who had discovered that a rogue CIA team in Frankfurt, called COREA, was protecting the drug route. According to a special report in *Time*, COREA used front companies for its overseas operations: Sevens

Mantra Corp, AMA Industries, Wilderwood Video and Condor Television Ltd. The report revealed that Condor did its banking through the First American Bank, a subsidiary of the Bank of Credit and Commerce International.

After explaining what he had learned to CIA headquarters in the U.S. and receiving no response, McKee decided to take his men home without the required permission. He planned to bring back to the U.S. proof of the rogue intelligence team's connection to Al-Kassar. If the government tried to cover it up, he would release his evidence to the press. Al-Kassar discovered this and reported McKee's attempt to make his own "travel arrangements" back to the U.S. through the rogue CIA team in Frankfurt. (*Covert Action*, Number 34, Summer 1990)

Although neglected in the American press, there were at least four, and possibly as many as eight, CIA and other U.S. intelligence agency operatives from Beirut aboard Pan-Am 103. (*Covert Action*, Number 34, Summer 1990) Could they have been the target? In his book *Lockerbie: The Tragedy of Flight 103*, David Johnson disclosed that CIA investigators removed a suitcase from the crash site that belonged to McKee. It was returned a few days later, and "found" empty.

The PBS investigative program *Frontline* reported in January 1990 that the bomb was put on the plane at London's Heathrow Airport where a baggage handler switched two suitcases belonging to CIA officer Mathew Gannon. According to the *Frontline* investigation, the only piece of luggage not accounted for from the flight belonged to Gannon.

Frontline claims that the intelligence officials were a "strong secondary target." A May 1989 report in the Arabic newspaper *Al-Dustur* revealed that McKee's team's movements were being monitored by David Lovejoy, an "American agent" who Aviv claims was passing information to the Iranian embassy in Beirut, telling the Iranian Charge d'affaires of the team's travel plans. (*Time*, April 27th, 1992)

Aviv believes that the CIA team in Frankfurt allowed Al-Kassar to continue to smuggle drugs into the U.S. in return for help in arranging the release of the American hostages. The drug operation, he says, went as far back as spring of 1987.

In the fall of 1988 the Syrian-based Popular Front for the Liberation of Palestine leader Ahmed Jibril, discovered the operation. So as not to interfere with Al-Kassar's activities, Jibril originally targeted an American Airlines, plane but the Mossad discovered this and tipped off the airline. When the plan changed and the target became a Pan-Am airliner, once again a Mossad agent tipped off German secret police 24 hours before the flight. When a BKA surveillance agent keeping watch over the suitcase supposedly filled with drugs noticed that this time the luggage was a different color and size, he passed this information on to the CIA team who relayed this to their superiors. They reportedly said "Don't worry about it. Don't stop it, let it go." (*Barron's*, December 17th, 1990)

Aviv says the BKA did just that. A lengthy article on Aviv's report in the financial weekly *Barron's* quotes one government Mideast Intelligence specialist as suggesting: "Do I think the CIA was involved? Of course they were involved. And they screwed up. Was the operation planned by the top? Probably not. I doubt they sanctioned heroin importation- that came about at the more zealous lower levels. But they knew what was going on and didn't care."

The expert went on to say that his agency had "things that support Aviv's allegation, but we can't prove it. We have no smoking gun. And until the other agencies of the government open their doors, we will have no smoking gun."

The other government agencies didn't open their doors. In September 1989, Pan-Am subpoenaed the FBI, CIA, FAA, DEA, National Security Council, National Security Agency, Defence Intelligence Agency and the State Department requesting documents relating to the case. According to Pan-Am's attorney Gregory Buhler, "the government quashed the subpoenas on grounds of national security." (*Barron's*, December 17th, 1990)

Further signs of a cover-up were revealed by investigative columnist Jack Anderson who claimed that President Bush and British Prime Minister Margaret Thatcher held a transatlantic phone conversation after Bush's inauguration in which they agreed that investigation into the case should be "limited" in order to avoid harming the two nations' intelligence communities. Thatcher has acknowledged that the conversation took place, but denied she and Bush conspired to interfere with the investigation. (*Covert Action*, Number 34, Summer 1990)

In its investigative report, *Time* revealed that a former agent for the Defence Intelligence Agency (DEA), Lester Knox Coleman III, has signed an affidavit which described the CIA-sanctioned operation. In 1987 Coleman was transferred to the Drug Enforcement Agency (DEA) and was assigned to Cyprus, where he witnessed the growing trade in heroin originating in Lebanon. Coleman's DEA front in Nicosia was Eurame Trading Co. Ltd., a firm located near the U.S. Embassy. It was his job was to keep track of al-Kasser's movements and report to the DEA attache in Cyprus, Michael Hurley. Coleman says he was paid in checks drawn on the BCCI branch in Luxembourg. (April 27th, 1992)

A number of investigative journalists believe that Aviv stumbled onto just one piece of a larger puzzle. In August 1991, Larry Cohler, a writer for the *Washington Jewish Week*, reported on a set of secret negotiations which took place between Syria and the United States government over the release of hostages, and which led to a number of covert trips by Bush to Damascus. Over an all-you-can-eat Indian lunch one afternoon, Larry told me an incredible story that compliments Aviv's conclusions.

According to confidential Pentagon memo that Cohler gained access to, for reasons still unknown, officials in the Reagan administration failed to pursue a series of Syrian offers to free the American hostages held in Lebanon. The Syrian overtures began in 1985 and continued through mid-1989. A number of former government officials involved in the secret Syrian negotiations say they were never told why the Syrian offers were not acted upon, while others claim that the Syrian offers were not genuine. Still others claim there was too little preliminary action by the U.S. government to determine for certain whether the initiatives were genuine or not. (*San Francisco Chronicle*, July 21st, 1991)

The center of the controversy was a memo dated March 17, 1987, which described a meeting attended by Lawrence Ropka Jr. a principal deputy of Assistant Secretary of Defence for National Security Affairs Richard Armitage. Written by Ropka's military assistant, Lt. Andrew Gambara, it claimed that American businessmen and a former executive secretary to Richard Nixon, Robert D. Ladd, told Pentagon officials in December 1985, that he had contact with a Lebanese businessman who introduced him to Fasih Makhail Ashi, a judge in the Syrian Inspector General's office. The judge claimed he had information regarding the fate of the seven American hostages held in Lebanon. Ashi said: "the Syrians were prepared to assist in the release of the hostages, if Reagan called Assad and requested his support." (*San Francisco Chronicle,* July 21, 1991)

Syrian's aims were simple enough. They wanted closer ties with the U.S. The memo said that once Reagan called, "Syria would facilitate the release and transfer of the hostages without any quid-pro-quo from the U.S." It said further that Ladd had already brought this to the attention of Oliver North at the NSC and that someone would follow it up. A former official in Armitage's office said the memo was sent to a special government agency, the Vice-President's Task Force on Terrorism, a group of high-ranking officials from the White House, State Department, NSC, and the CIA.

Two of Armitages' aides acknowledged that the Syrian initiative was discussed during a number of interviews with Ladd and his attorney. Ladd said that after hearing the Syrian offer he arranged for Ashi to come to the U.S. and be questioned over a period of a number of days by the Task Force. Ashi asserts that he spoke in the name of General Ghaza Kenan, head of Syrian Military Intelligence, and even passed on details about the fate of the kidnapped CIA chief in Beirut, William Buckley.

Ashi returned to Syria but received no reply. In February 1987 he contacted Ladd and again said Syria would help the Americans release the hostages. Ladd tried unsuccessfully to persuade government officials to meet in Paris with Ashi. A long-time senior aide to Armatage claimed Ashi could not prove the offer was genuine. "It was my sense there was nothing there," he said, "I was told there wasn't enough information from Ashi to run it upstairs." (*San Francisco Examiner*, July 21st, 1991)

However a former official in Armatage's office said that he thought Ashi's overtures should at least be checked out, as the American government could have easily sent someone from the

Paris embassy to meet him. Ladd said that it was only because of his persistence that U.S. intelligence officials eventually agreed to meet with Ashi. Then, in the early part of the summer of 1989 the CIA, without any explanation, cancelled the meeting.

Despite the cancellation, Ashi called Ladd back saying that the hostages would be released if Ladd would come to Damascus for them. In August Ladd was prepared to fly to Damascus when Ashi called back to withdraw the offer, saying that a tug of war over releasing the hostages had developed between Kenen and other factions of the Syrian army.

The Congressional investigators did look into why the Administration didn't follow-up on these initiatives and why Syria's offer to help release the hostages was put on hold. They questioned a number of individuals, including a former Pentagon official, Peter Probst, who took part in some of the meetings. He told Cohler that this was one of several meetings that he and other officials had with Ladd about the Syrian overture. He would say nothing further about the matter.

Could the Administration have been pursuing another path to free the hostages? Cohler learned from different sources that Bush made as many as four secret trips to Damascus in early 1986, allegedly offering arms to Syria in return for the hostages. Congressional investigators were told by their sources that in the spring of 1988, in the middle of the presidential campaign, Bush made one final trip to Syria telling the Syrians that the time was right to make a deal. Then, the Syrians stalled.

At that point the Syrians might have grasped the leverage they actually had over Bush and have wanted to up the ante. (*In These Times*, August 7th, 1991) It's also possible that Bush might have been attempting an "October Surprise" of his own by having the hostages delivered to a Republican White House just in time for the Presidential election in November 1988.

Aviv says that when these overtures failed, Bush and the CIA turned to Al-Kassar as a middleman. A covert deal made with drug smugglers is, after all, less likely to be exposed than one with a government or head of state. Al-Kassar had some experience in these types of operations and at least one victory under his belt: he was used by the French government in March 1988 to free its own hostages held in captivity in Lebanon. George Bush, may have wanted the same deal.

What Is a Covert Operation?

"A covert operation is, in its nature, a lie."
Oliver North in his
testimony before the
Iran- Contra congres-
sional investigations

The major problem investigative journalists have
in determining the secret agenda behind covert
operations is the secrecy which surrounds these
activities. Gary Sick discovered this during his
investigation into the "October Surprise" scandal.

"For those conducting a covert action, there
are three layers of protection against disclosure,"
he says. "First, there is the culture of secrecy surrounding such operations. People are sworn to
silence, and they take their oaths with the utmost
seriousness. Second, there is compartmentaliza-
tion. Ideally, in a covert action almost no one

should have the whole picture. Especially those at a lower level should have as little information as possible about any activities except those required to fulfill their mission. The third layer of protection is culpability. If the covert operation involves criminal actions, the source will be reluctant to subject himself to possible prosecution. That inhibition is greatly strengthened if those he is accusing happen to be in positions of great political power" (*October Surprise: America's Hostages in Iran and the Election of Ronald Reagan*).

These layers of protection pose a major obstacle to journalists seeking to expose a covert operation. Sick points out that the "need to know" is the rule, and if it is rigorously observed, even a disgruntled operative will only be able to reveal one tiny dimension of the operation. Thus, even exposing one aspect of the adventure, doesn't reveal the wider secret agenda.

"If the operative is also a suspect character, which is typically the case, then deniability is even easier to maintain, since he can easily be discredited by the 'respectable' people who planned the operation."

For these reasons, most covert operations never get discovered. The covert operations that are exposed are usually the unsuccessful ones that screw up.

Robert Senci

Whatever Robert Senci was involved in before he was arrested is a good example of a covert operation that wasn't successful, became public, but still didn't expose the wider secret agenda it was supporting.

During the summer of 1991, I became good friends with William Northrup. He was arrested along with Israeli General Avraham Baram in Bermuda in April 1986 and was illegally deported to the United States on trumped-up charges of "conspiracy" to defraud the U.S. government. He gave me Bobby Senci's number and told me to call him. "Bobby's part of the Brown Helmut Society," said Northrup, using the term to refer to those in the Iran-Contra Affair who went to jail for merely carrying out the orders of their superiors. "The ones that got dumped on," Northrup liked to say.

On March 22nd, 1988, Robert Mario Senci was found guilty by a Washington, D.C., court of six counts of mail fraud, four counts of first-degree theft, and eleven counts of interstate transportation of stolen securities. His lawyer told the jury he was authorized to spend the $2.5 million he was accused of stealing by a high-ranking Kuwaiti Airlines official who was also a member of the Kuwaiti royal family.

Senci was involved in a covert operation that to this day has yet to be exposed. By going to jail rather than opening his mouth, Senci was simply abiding by the rules set down for covert operators. "If you get caught, you go down and keep your trap shout," Northrup would tell me.

From 1977 until his arrest in 1986, Senci was the local sales manager in Washington for Kuwaiti Airlines, a perfect cover for his covert activities. According to testimony given during the trial, he took payments sent by the airline to the cultural division of the Kuwaiti Embassy in Washington and deposited them in several bank accounts. Kuwaiti Airlines officials testified that Senci was not authorized to maintain the account.

Senci claimed most of the money was spent on a mission by the CIA to forge ties with moderates in Iran who would ultimately be spying for the agency. The plan, Senci said, was approved by the Kuwaiti government because of its own vulnerability to Iranian Islamic fundamentalism.

The CIA admitted that it had a "relationship" with Senci from late 1983 until the time of his arrest. Robert Carter, as former aide to CIA director William Casey, wrote a letter to the judge on Senci's behalf, saying, "I know that Mr. Senci was often involved in highly technical and extremely important meetings around the world. These meetings on many occasions were held to further the interests of the United States government."

Although he faced a ten-year prison sentence, Senci was given only six months. Before being arrested, Senci told the court: "I solemnly swear before the court, and to almighty God, that I am a patriot and that what I did was for my country and fellow man."

What did Senci do? In an exclusive interview in the *Village Voice* (July 23rd, 1991), Senci says he worked closely with CIA Director William Casey in "Republicans Abroad," an organization created to further Republican Party goals abroad. A front for covert activity would be a better description for it, as it was used, for example, for a CIA operation to recruit Iranian spies and to gain information on Americans being held hostage in Lebanon. It enabled Senci to get close to potential spies in the Iranian community in Europe.

Senci says he worked with Carter and was also a consultant for the powerful Washington lobbying firm of Robert Gray Ltd., known for its close ties to the Administration and U.S. intelligence bodies. (In November 1983, Robert Owen, an aide to then-Senator Dan Quayle and Oliver North's co-operator of the Contra supply operation, began working for Gray and Co. to improve the image of the Contras in Congress.) Says Senci: "Gray was also the chief lobbyist for the Kuwaiti government to encourage the U.S. to go to war in the Persian Gulf in November and December 1990."

In what might have become a second Iran-Contra, in late 1985, Habib Moallem, an Iranian contact of Sensi's, proposed that Iran would trade oil and the American hostages in return for U.S. help in reconstructing its oil refineries, which had been bombed by the Iraqis. He says the proposal was the brainchild of William Wilson, the U.S. Ambassador to the Vatican, who arranged for Senci and Moallem to meet Vice President Bush, Casey, and a number of people from Robert Gray's lobbying firm. The meeting got leaked to the press and never took place, but plans were drawn up by Casey, Senci, and Carter to initiate the deal.

CIA IS THE USA

How the CIA and Intelligence Community Became the Major Instrument of U.S Policy

How did President Bush do it? How did he implement secret agendas, lie about his role in Iran-Contra, sucker Saddam Hussein and the American people into the Gulf War, without anybody catching on?

The answer lies in Bush's ideological underpinnings and view of how the world should be run.

Bush's talk of a "New World Order" isn't so new at all. It comes straight from the ideology of the Skull and Bones society, which believes that its members have a strategic and moral obligation (i.e., right) to control the events of the world. Their goal is to restore the "greatness of America" in world affairs, since they see themselves as a distinguished WASP caste, a modern-day version of the Roman warrior.

The Order of Skull and Bones, one of seven secret elite fraternal societies based at Yale University in New Haven, Connecticut, allows only 15 males in their junior year to join. Potential selectees must be white, male and wealthy. Non-WASPS are excluded. If a woman were ever allowed into the Skull and Bones meeting place, the clubhouse would have to be bulldozed (*Esquire*, September 1977).

"Bonesmen," as they are called, believe in the notion of "constructive chaos," which justifies covert actions to "maintain order." To confuse the public they employ ambiguity and secrecy, i.e., disinformation. Thus the foreign policies of Bonesmen who hold public office are almost always carried out via a secret agenda through the instrument of covert operations.

Anthony Sutton, an historian who has written a book on the Order, says that since its founding it has taken on more occult and ritualistic trappings and that it is secretly known among its members as the "Brotherhood of Death." Others claim the society's Germanic origins are reflected in the building on the Yale campus that the secret order uses, which is said to contain remnants of Hitler's private collection of silver dinnerware and Barvarian tea-pots.

The 15 new members selected each year go through a formal initiation ceremony. The senior members of the Order come to their door, knock three times, then tap the potential member on the shoulder and ask: "Skull and Bones: Do you accept?" If the candidate accepts, a message wrapped with a black ribbon sealed by black wax with the skull and crossbones emblem is handed to the inductee. This will tell him when and where to meet on initiation night.

According to a 1940 Skull and Bones document, the initiation ceremony consists of the potential member being placed in a coffin, buried six feet under, then chanted over in Latin for the better part of an hour. The inductee, more than a little grateful to be returned from a burial alive, is then dug up and reborn into the society. He is then removed from the coffin and given a robe with symbols on it. A bone with his name on it will be tossed into the bone heap at the start of every meeting.

Historically, "Bonesmen" have had a tremendous influence on American foreign policy. Alphonso Taft, a co-founder of Skull and Bones, was Secretary of War in 1876 and Attorney General in 1876-1877. He brought pressure on President William McKinley to enter the war against Spain to "liberate" Cuba and seize the Philippines. When McKinley was assassinated in Buffalo, New York, Bonesman Teddy Roosevelt moved into the White House and surrounded himself with fellow Bonesmen such as William Howard Taft, who later became his hand picked successor for the Republican nomination and was elected President in 1908 (*Covert Action*, No. 33, Winter 1990).

Other "Bonesmen" include: Robert Taft, Speaker of the House in 1921-1926 and Senator from Ohio, 1938-1950; Robert Lovett, Assistant Secretary of War 1941-1945, Deputy Secretary of Defense, and Secretary of Defense in 1950; Averell Harriman, U.S. Ambassador to the Soviet Union, 1943-1946, Governor of New York and then Under Secretary of State for Asia, 1961-1963; General George Marshall, Chief of Staff during World War II who would later serve as Harry Truman's Secretary of State; William Bundy, Stimson's special assistant at the War Department (one of Bundy's sons, McGorge, was President Kennedy's and Johnson's National Security Advisor; the other, William, was a CIA official and served in the Departments of State and Defense); William F. Buckley, Jr., the founder of the *National Review*, and his brother James, who served, 1981-1982, in the Reagan White House as Under Secretary of State for Security Assistance, Science and Technology (*Covert Action*, No. 33, Winter 1990). Along with George Bush, highly placed Bonesmen serving under the Republican aegis include James Lilley, U.S. Ambassador to Beijing, and David Boren, chairman of the Senate Intelligence Committee, a Democrat from Oklahoma.

Godfrey Hodgson, foreign editor of *The Independent* of London and author of *The Colonel: The Life and Wars of Henry Stimson 1867-1950* (1990), says that George Bush's mentor was "Bonesman" Henry Stimson, who was Secretary of State under Hoover and served in the Roosevelt and Truman cabinets. "Stimson contributed enormously to Bush's political development," writes Hodgson. "It was the "most important educational experience in his life" (*The Nation*, January 21st, 1991).

Early "Bonesmen" were internationalists (i.e., imperialists) who believed that the U.S. would and should play a great role in the world's destiny through the twentieth century. Stimson thought it was imperative for America to dominate the Pacific Ocean and Far East. It was this imperialistic ideology which encouraged President McKinley to enter the Spanish-American War.

Stimson served under six presidents: Theodore Roosevelt, William Howard Taft, Woodrow Wilson, Calvin Coolidge, Franklin Roosevelt and

Harry Truman. He oversaw the Manhattan Project and personally decided to use atomic weapons against Japan, as well as formulating Herbert Hoover's military and economic restrictions against Japan in the postwar era.

Bush was brought up in the Stimson tradition that the U.S. was - circa 1890 to 1950 - a great power. He learned from Stimson, says Hodgson, that "the task of the leader is not to negotiate or prevaricate, but rather to stay firm, draw a line in the sand, and, if that line is crossed, to fight" (*The Nation*).

Stimson believed that America needed to enter into a military confrontation every thirty years or so. This, he contended, enabled a nation to rally behind the flag and gave it a common sense of purpose. In one fell swoop, the failures of previous decades could be wiped clean. The Gulf War served that purpose for President Bush.

Armed with the Skull and Bones ideology, Bush needed a vehicle in the Reagan-Bush White House to carry out a covert foreign policy. That instrument was "The Vice President's Task Force on Combating Terrorism," which was followed by the National Security Decision Directive Number 3, giving Bush responsibility for the "Crisis Management Committee" in the Cabinet (*New York Times*, April 12th, 1981). Then came the "The Terrorist Incident Working Group," created to bring back hostages held in Lebanon, and finally the "Operations Sub-Group" and the "Restricted Terrorist Incidents Working Group."

By establishing a special apparatus, the Vice President's Task Force on Combating Terrorism, Bush and Casey created a network which was able to bypass normal channels and initiate policies that might have been opposed by other White House officials such as Secretary of State Schultz and Secretary of Defense Weinberger (*Covert Action*, No. 33, Winter 1990).

The members of the Task Force were: Robert Oakley (then director of the State Department's Office to Combat Terrorism), Charles Allen, Robert Earl, and middle-level operatives at the CIA such as Duane Clarride, Ray Clines, and Charles Allen, as well as Noel Koch from the Defense Department, Lt. General John Moellering from the Joint Chiefs of Staff, Executive Assistant of the FBI Oliver Revell, Lt. General Sam Wilson and Lt. General Harold Aaron, both former Directors of the Defense Intelligence Agency, General Richard Stillwell, former CIA Chief of Covert Operations in the Far East, and Deputy Director of the CIA Robert Gates. (It's interesting to note that despite Bush leading the Task Force on Combating Terrorism, the great threat of terrorism which the American people heard so much about during the Reagan

Administration seems to have disappeared in the Bush White House.)

Members of the Task Force used counter-terrorism channels to thwart official U.S. policy if they disapproved of it and to conceal their activities from their superiors. They were the operatives who moved the policies from the Task Force Senior Review Group and executed them, with the collaboration of among others Oliver North, through the Operations Sub-Group (*Covert Action*, No. 33, Winter 1990). They were Bush's secret team of covert operators.

"Probably the worst thing for society is to have a head of state who is also a former covert operator," says former CIA operative Victor Marchetti. "During these times the secret services get out of control."

The Reagan-Bush White House: A New Era in Secret Government

As early as March 1981 the Reagan-Bush Administration paved the way for a new wave of covert operations. After Watergate, Presidents Ford and Carter tried to issue executive orders to curb CIA activities, particularly ones which involved the violation of the civil liberties of American citizens. Yet a blue ribbon commission established in 1975 headed by Vice President Nelson Rockefeller, and coincidentally with Ronald Reagan (then Govenor of California) as a member, concluded that "Presidents should refrain from directing the CIA to perform what are essentially internal security tasks."

A proposal put forth by the Bush-Reagan Administration as early as March 23rd, 1981, drafted by mid-level career agents, permitted the agency to undertake covert operations within the U.S. and to spy on American citizens. The new order no longer required the CIA to collect information by the "least intrusive means possible," and so enabled the CIA to regularly conduct searches without warrants, surreptitious entries, and infiltration of political organizations (*Time*, March 23rd, 1981).

The push for the executive order was made under the guise of combating terrorism. In the early meetings of the National Security Council, it was argued that limits put on the CIA prevented the agency from conducting surveillance on suspected terrorists once they had entered the country. (How many terrorist attacks took place in the United States during the 1970s? No-one thought to ask.)

Some members of Congress didn't like the new regulations. Don Edwards, then chairman of the House Civil and Constitutional Rights Subcommittee, said the draft order would "put the CIA back in the business of domestic spying" (*Time*, March 23rd, 1981).

The Bush-Reagan Administration used another technique to create the political framework for its string of secret agendas and covert operations. Writing in June 1989 in *The Nation*, Eve Pell, a staff reporter at the Center for Investigative Reporting in San Francisco, described how secret presidential decrees and National Security Decision Directives (NSDD) had propelled America into some of the controversial events of the previous decade. President Reagan issued nearly 300 NSDDs. It was an NSDD that enabled the CIA to begin arming Contra soldiers, and that arming was part of the build-up which resulted in the invasion of Grenada in 1983.

An NSDD is not like an executive order or presidential finding, as the latter are made known to the the House and Senate Intelligence committees, whereas NSDDs do not have to be revealed to any other branch of government. Of the 300 NSDDs issued by Reagan, less than fifty have been declassified in whole or in part by the National Security Council, the one government body which decides if an NSDD will be made public. In other words, only 15 percent of the most important policy decisions made during the Bush-Reagan White House are known to the American people.

Allan Adler, a former legislative counsel to the American Civil Liberties Union, said the Reagan-Bush Administration "had a pronounced proclivity for using NSDDs, apparently because it didn't have to make them public." Anna Nelson, an historian at Tulane University, says that the Reagan White House was "extraordinary in its abuse of the process." "The original National Security

Council documents were broad policy papers, with agency implementation," she also explained. "Some of Reagan's NSDDs bypassed even normal agency channels, as well as Congress. The arrogance of this arrangement is incredible."

Eve Pell argues that during the Reagan Administration, the NSDDs were the backbone of the hidden government, issued to evade congressional scrutiny and on certain occasions ordering actions which stand in direct contradiction to the then publicly stated policy of the government.

NSDD Number 77 is a good example of how Bush and Reagan employed NSDDs to serve secret agenda goals. It allowed the National Security Council to coordinate inter-agency efforts for what was called the "Management of Public Diplomacy Relative to National Security." This directive served as a the basis for "public diplomacy activities" (i.e., propaganda) by enabling "organizational support for foreign governments and private groups to encourage the growth of democratic political institutions and practices." In reality, the directive created mini-propaganda ministries operating out of the National Security Council, the State Department and the White House. The General Accounting Office believed these activities violated the law banning "covert propaganda" within the U.S.

In 1987, then head of the House Government

Operations Committee Jack Brooks asked National Security advisor Frank Carlucci for a list of all the NSDDs issued by the Reagan Administration since 1981. Carlucci refused and called into the question the constitutionality of the request. Speaker of the House Jim Wright, after being denied access to the same list, claimed "Congress cannot react responsibly to new dictates for national policy set in operation by the executive branch behind closed doors."

Brooks was unable to pass a bill requiring that the Speaker of the Senate be informed of any new NSDDs. At the hearing on that bill, Representative Louis Stokes asked "Is the secret policy of the United States the same as the public policy of the United States . . with respect to very sensitive matters such as terrorism and paramilitary covert actions?"

George Bush, Donald Gregg and Iran-Contra: What Did They Know?

George Bush would have preferred that all of the policies and covert operations he initiated remain secret. When they didn't, he and his staff simply denied their existence, or their involvement in them. To set the historical record straight, it's important to look at George Bush's entire repertoire of official responses to all of the scandals which came under the umbrella of what became commonly known as the "Iran-Contra Affair."

Bush insisted that he was "out of the loop" on all matters relating to Iran-Contra. He came to understand the "hidden dimensions" of the scandal only in December 1986 after his National Security Advisor, Donald Gregg, briefed him. This was nearly a month after Attorney General Edwin

Meese disclosed the diversion of arms sales profits to the Contras. "Not until that briefing," Bush says, "did I fully appreciate how the initiative was actually implemented."

What is Bush trying to tell us? That secret, covert operations are going on and the highest elected officials in the country are not informed of them? That would indicate either a silent coup, or an extremely poor grasp on national affairs on the part of the President and Vice President.

Logic would dictate that Bush would have had to know what was going on. He admitted that he attended a meeting on August 6th, 1985, when former National Security Advisor Robert McFarlane outlined the deal to trade U.S. arms for American hostages held by the Iranians. On January 6th, 1986, President Reagan authorized the sale of TOW missiles to win the release of the American hostages. The next morning all of the President's advisors gathered in the Oval Office as Secretary of State George Schultz and Secretary of Defense Caspar Weinberger expressed their opposition. Schultz told the Tower Commission that by the end of the meeting it was clear that the President and the Vice President disagreed with him (Schultz). A few weeks later, National Security Advisor John Poindexter sent a computer message to North which acknowledged high-level opposition to his policies, but concluded: "President and V.P. are solid in taking the position that we have to try."

What was Bush's response to this meeting? "I may have been out of the room at the time and didn't recall the two Secretaries' strenuous opposition." Bush claims that if he had heard them he would have "moved to reconsider the whole project."

By his own response, at the very least Bush knew there was a "project." He would like the American people to believe that throughout discussion of the most controversial issues of the Reagan White House's foreign policy agenda by the President and his top advisors, George was out of the room taking a leak.

Amiram Nir, advisor on terrorism to former Israeli Prime Minister Shimon Peres, met Bush in the King David Hotel in Jerusalem on July 29th, 1986. According to notes taken by Craig Fuller, Bush's aide, Nir outlined for Bush all efforts taken throughout the preceding year "to gain the release of the hostages, and pointed out that the decision remained as to whether the arms desired by the Iranians would be delivered in separate shipments or for each hostage as they are released." "We are dealing with the most radical elements," Nir told Bush, according to the memorandum published in the Tower Commission Report, despite Reagan administration officials effort to quash it.

President Bush said that "he couldn't remember much about the briefing, nor did he fully understand what Nir was saying at the time." (Was Nir speaking in Hebrew?) He said, "I didn't know what he was referring to when he was talking about radicals, nor did I ask."

Why then didn't the VP say to himself, "Hey, if these activities are being carried out by a foreign government and involve the sale of American-made weapons to secure the release of U.S. citizens, I need to know all the details," and then ask Nir for a full explanation of the events?" If he didn't like what he was hearing, why didn't he demand that the entire operation be called off? If Bush had no idea what Nir was talking about, why was he meeting him? What did his advisors, who arranged the meeting with Nir, brief Bush on, that was going to be discussed, if not arms for hostages?

In another comment Bush responded, "I listened to him [Nir] and there was not a big exchange in all of this. I did not know all the details. I didn't know what he was referring to when he was talking about "radicals." Asked why he didn't raise questions on the initiative, Bush responded by saying he felt "uncomfortable" at the meeting and thought it was a "listening session" (*Washington Post*, October 21st, 1988).

What does that mean? That Bush felt "uncomfortable" speaking to Nir about a secret effort to release U.S. hostages, or about selling American weapons to a country that supposedly America hates and considers a terrorist threat. What does he mean by a "listening session"? Listening to what? Nir's views on Third World economic development? When did Bush believe it was going to become a "doing session"?

On the campaign trail in July 1988, Bush said, "Nir presented him with only a tiny piece of a very complicated puzzle." Does that mean Nir told gave him details of the arms for hostages deal but George couldn't complete the "puzzle"?

Bush is asking the American people to believe that the Vice President of the United States took time out of a busy two-day state visit to meet with Israel's official counterterrorism expert, a subject on which Bush headsed a high-level inter-agency group at the White House. But when they speak, he has no interest in what Nir is saying. He doesn't bother to ask Nir to clarify his references or thoughts, instead he ust sits and listens, but hasn't a clue to what Nir is talking about because Bush knows nothing of any efforts to free hostages. Bush then stands up, shakes his head because he hasn't understood a word this person has told him, announces that he doesn't want to hear any more, and walks out of the room.

Did Bush Know of the Operation to Supply the Contras?

Bush's official response to what he knew of the secret effort to supply the Nicaraguan Contras is more complicated. Here, his National Security Advisor, Donald Gregg, saves his boss from having to answer any questions by insisting that Bush didn't know about any of these initiatives. He claims he didn't tell Bush about any of these activities because "he didn't think it was Vice Presidential" enough for Bush to know. Thus, Bush never knew.

Is such a contention believable? Is it possible that the Vice President's chief aide was fully informed of all activities to arm and train the Contras, but that his boss, the Vice President, wasn't? Why would Gregg want to keep these important security matters a secret from his boss? Deniability? Did Bush tell Gregg, "Since Congress won't let us support the Contras, you have to find a way to keep them supplied with weapons. Do whatever you have to do, just don't tell me about it so I will be able to claim I didn't know"? If so, this means that at the very least Bush knew about the existence of these secret operations and is guilty of violating a congressional ban.

Efforts by the Vice President's Office to supply the Contras begin in the summer of 1982 when Bush and Casey met and came up with the Black Eagle Operation, a plan to ship weapons to the Contras through San Antonio, Texas, to Panama and from there on to El Salvador (*Rolling Stone*, November 3rd, 1988). According to a retired army covert operative assigned to the operation, Bush agreed to use his office as a cover while Gregg coordinated financial and operational details. "Bush and Gregg were the asbestos wall," says the retired military man. "You had to burn through them to get to Casey" (*Rolling Stone*, November 3rd, 1988).

A memo dated March 17th, 1983, written by Gregg to then-National Security Advisor Bud McFarlane, describes how former CIA operative Felix Rodriguez, who served under Donald Gregg in Vietnam, had devised a military plan called "Pink Team" to launch mobile air strikes with "minimum U.S. participation" against leftist rebels in Central America. The plan was never implemented, but Rodriguez was soon after recruited full-time into the effort to resupply the Contras.

When asked, after he gave sworn testimony to Iran-Contra investigators, why he had failed to mention this secret memo, Gregg replied, "One, I didn't think of it. Two, it had nothing to do with the questions being asked of me." In those same hearings, he testified: "We [Bush and Gregg] never discussed the Contras. We had no responsibility for it; we had no expertise in it." Also in 1983 the Vice President's Office dispatched Gustavo Villoldo, former CIA agent in Honduras and Bay of Pigs veteran, to work as a combat advisor and to establish an arms supply line to the Contras. According to former intelligence agents who claim they worked with the VP's office, Villoldo was one of several individuals recruited by Gregg to work outside normal CIA channels (*The Progressive*, May 1987).

In November 1983 the National Security Council (of which Bush was a member) needed to find more weapons for the Contras. One of North's memos stated that Bush had been asked to "concur on these [weapons] increases in each previous case" (*Rolling Stone*, November 3rd, 1988).

In an eleven-point memo to his boss on September 18th, 1984, entitled "Funding for the Contras" and made available to Iran-Contra investigators, Gregg discussed military and political aspects of the Contra war. He told Bush, "In response to your question, Dewey Clarridge supplied the following information: A very tough estimate would be that they [the Contras] have received about $1.5 million [from private sources]. This is based on what we know of Contra purchases of gasoline, ammunition, etc." (*The Progressive*, March 1987).

For ten months in 1985 an operation known as the "Arms Supermarket" supplied the Contras. It consisted of private arms merchants tied to the CIA, as well as the intelligence arms of the Honduras military, and was financed in part with money from the Medellín cocaine cartel (*Rolling Stone*, November 3rd, 1988).

In April 1988 the Senate Foreign Relations Subcommittee on Narcotics, Terrorism and International Operations, headed by Senator John Kerry, heard testimony from Richard Brenneke, who worked for the CIA on the project. Brenneke said that Gregg was the Washington contact for the operation and that he (Brenneke) made numerous purchases of arms manufactured in the Eastern Bloc. Brenneke further claimed that Noriega granted transit privileges for the flights and took his own cut of the profits.

Bush responded to allegations that his office was involved in the operation by personally accusing Senator Kerry of allowing "slanderous" allegations to leak from his committee, and insisted that the newsmagazine *Newsweek*, which published details of the operation, was printing "garbage." Despite the fact that Brenneke was not charged with any crime, Bush said, "The guy whom they are quoting is the guy who is trying to save his own neck (*Washington Post*, May 17th, 1988).

Another incident Bush denied involvement in was having offered a *quid pro quo* to Honduran President Roberto Suazo Córdova in return for his help in training the Contras. A memo written by John Poindexer on February 20th, 1985, reads: "We want the VP [Bush] to discuss these matters with Suazo" (*Time*, May 15th, 1989).

Bush paid a visit to Tegucigalpa on March 16th, 1985, and met with President Roberto Suazo Córdova, promising him that the U.S. would increase military and economic aid in return for his help in aiding the Contras. Bush assured the Honduran government that it could expect to be rewarded if it continued to harbor Contra camps on its territory and supply military goods to the rebels. This was at the point when Córdova was threatening to close down the camps and stop all arms shipments.

That *quid pro quo* was approved the previous month at a meeting of the Special Interagency Crisis-Planning group Bush headed (*Time*, April 17, 1989). While aid began almost immediately after Bush's visit, as did Honduran support for the Contras, Bush would still contend at a photo session after he had become President that "the word of the President of the United States, George Bush, is, There was no *quid pro quo*. No implication, no *quid pro quo*, direct or indirect, from me to the President of Honduras. There has been much needless, mindless speculation about my word of honor, and I've answered it now, definitely" (*Time*, May 15th, 1989). (No, George, you didn't answer it. You simply denied it.) But if it wasn't a *quid pro quo* and Bush didn't discuss Contra business with Suazo Córdova, what was so important that the VP had to make a personal trip to Honduras? A tourist exchange?

Also in 1985 Gregg sent Felix Rodriguez to El Salvador to aid the Contra resupply effort. General Paul Gorman, then head of U.S. military forces in Central America, wrote a memo to the U.S. ambassador in El Salvador. In it he said: "Rodriquez is operating as a private citizen but his acquaintanceship with the VP is real enough, going back to the latter days of DCI [Director of Central Intelligence]" (*The Progressive*, March 1989).

While Gorman knew the purpose behind Rodriquez's presence in El Salvador, Gregg claimed he didn't, contending that all he knew was that Rodriguez was sent to El Salvador "to deal with insurgency." When asked why Rodriguez would tell his plans to Gorman but not to Gregg, Gregg replied, "Felix doesn't tell me everything he does. I just had never heard of it". (*The Progressive*, March 1987).

Gregg, however, does admit he met with Felix Rodriguez, but said they never discussed the

Contras. He maintained that Rodriguez didn't mention his work with the Contras because he knew that "that was not my interest." Gregg is saying Rodriguez may have been working on an operation to supply the Contras, but it wasn't on behalf of the Vice President's Office. That it must have been a private initiative by Rodriguez which was not sanctioned by the U.S. government; therefore it would not "be in Gregg's interest."

Bush's ties to Rodriguez and Latin American drug lords were confirmed by Ramón Milián Rodríguez, a financier for the Medellín drug cartel who is currently serving a 43-year prison sentence and therefore has nothing to gain by lying. Rodríguez testified before a Senate investigation into ties between the Contras and drug traffickers. He told the PBS documentary program *Frontline*: "Guns, Drugs and the CIA" that he received a request for $10 million from Felix Rodriguez to finance Contra support: "The request for the contribution made a lot more sense because Felix was reporting to George Bush. If Felix had come to me and said I'm not reporting to anyone else, let's say, you know, Oliver North, I might have been more skeptical. I didn't know who Oliver North was and I didn't know his background. But if you have a CIA, or what you consider to be a CIA-man, coming to you saying, 'I want to fight this war, we're out of funds, can you help us out?

I'm reporting directly to Bush on it',' I mean it's very real, very believable, here you have a CIA guy reporting to his old boss."

For two guys who rose to the highest levels of the political echelons in the United States, Gregg and Bush sure have bad memories. In Oliver North's notebooks there is an entry from September 10th, 1985, which discusses a meeting he had with Donald Gregg and the chief of the U.S. military advisory group in El Salvador, Colonel James Steele. The three discussed "logistic support" for the Contras. When asked about the meeting, Gregg simply said: "I don't think that meeting ever took place" (*Newsweek*, May 23rd, 1986). A handwritten note dated November 1985 from George Bush to Oliver North thanked North for his "dedication and tireless work with the hostage thing and with Central America." When asked later about the note, Bush said "he didn't recall why he sent it." (What other reason could Bush have had to send it other than to thank North for his efforts? Does Bush not remember anything to do with "the hostage thing" or "Central America"?

What would happen to a doctor who told the jury during a malpractice suit against him that "he forgot" to tell his patient there would be side effects to the drug he prescribed for him? Why can a doctor be sued for malpractice of his profession but a national leader can just say he forgot, and no further investigation is required?

In a April 1986 meeting on supplying the Contras, Rodriguez complained to Gregg that North's men were skimming profit from the arms sales. When asked about this meeting, Gregg said he didn't tell Bush about Rodriguez's complaints because it wasn't "Vice-Presidential." Gregg's response indicates that he knew about the operation to arm the Contras, from at least April 1986 onwards. It could also be inferred that Bush knew, but that Gregg didn't want to inform him of Rodriguez's complaints.

Gregg's aide, Colonel Samuel Watson, wrote two memos before attending a May 1986 meeting with Bush and Gregg which briefed Bush on "the status of the war in El Salvador and the resupply of the Contras." When asked how it was that he could deny knowing anything about supplying the Contras when that meeting apparently discussed those very topics, Gregg admitted he was "baffled as to how that agenda item appears.... It was possible that it was a garbled reference to resupply of copters instead of resupply of Contras," he explained (UPI, May 13th, 1989).

When Colonel Watson was asked by Iran-Contra investigators about the role of the Vice President's Office in the Contra effort, he answered: "I've taken it as assumed that it was my duty that anything to do with Nicaragua or Central America that came through the Office of the Vice President was of interest to us because the Vice President is a principal of the National Security Council. Dealing with the Contras would be among my responsibilities." Contra leader Eden Pastora said in a sworn deposition in July 1987 that Bush was in the "Contra resupply chain of command" (*The Nation*, January 23rd, 1988).

In August 1986 Gregg had a meeting with Rodriguez at which he was told about a scheme to "swap weapons for dollars to get aid for the Contras." When asked about his own hand-written notes on the meeting, Gregg claimed he "didn't know what that line meant," and that "he didn't tell his boss about the meeting because it wasn't Vice-Presidential material." (Probably the most vital national securty issue of the day, but Gregg didn't think it was important enough to disturb the Vice-President over.)

At his confirmation hearing for the office of ambassador to South Korea in 1989, Senator Alan Cranston, then chairman of the Foreign Relations Subcommittee on East Asian and Pacific Affairs, became fed up with Gregg's constant denials about the Contra resupply effort, and eventually shouted at him: "Your career training in establishing secrecy and deniability for covert operations and your decades-old friendship with Felix

Rodriguez apparently led you to believe that you could serve the national interest by sponsoring a freelance operation out of the Vice President's Office" (*New York Times*, May 13th, 1989).

When Cranston inquiredhow it could be possible that Gregg didn't know that Rodriguez was involved with an operation to supply the Contras, Gregg replied that Oliver North and Rodriguez must have been "conspiring against him." When North testified at his trial that it was Gregg who introduced him to Rodriguez, Gregg said North's statements were "just not true" (*Los Angeles Times*, May 13th 1989).

Even after Eugene Hasenfus, who was flying arms to the Contras on one of Secord's C-123 planes, was shot down on October 5th, 1986 over southern Nicaragua, Gregg said he still didn't tell Bush about the operation. (Apparently, the Vice President didn't have a minute free on his busy calendar to deal with such mundane affairs.)

Asked about reports of the downed plane's ties to the VP's office, and that the first telephone call Hasenfus made was to the Vice President's staff, Bush said: "It's absolutely, totally untrue. I can deny it unequivocally" (*The Progressive*, May 1987). When *Newsweek* queried him on February 8th, 1988, about the incident, Bush replied: "I am told that Colonel Watson canvassed appropriate officials in the U.S. government and was informed that the missing airplane did not belong to the U.S. government, was not on a U.S. government operation and that the missing person was not a U.S. government employee. Based on the definitive statements from responsible officials, Colonel Watson set aside the fragmentary information Mr. Rodriguez had given him and took the word of the U.S. officials that there was no U.S. government connection."

In plain English, Bush is saying that the entire effort to resupply the Contras was a totally private affair, with no connection to or foreknowledge by the White House.

When press reports of telephone records from Rodriguez's safe in San Salvador showed a number of calls to the White House and Gregg's home, on December 15th, 1986, Bush's office acknowledged that Gregg and Rodriquez had discussed Contra-aid, and that Colonel Watson had been called by Rodriguez and told the Hasenfus flight was missing¾a full day before the downing was announced by the Nicaraguan government" (*The Progressive*, May 1987). A statement released by the Vice President's Office said that "Gregg and his staff maintained periodic communications with Felix Rodriguez, but were never involved in directing, coordinating, or approving military aid to the Contras in Nicaragua" (*The Progressive*, May 1987). The Vice President insisted that these contacts concerned El Salvador, not the Contras.

When interviewed on the CBS news program *60 Minutes* in March 1987, the Vice President replied that these statements had "stood the test of time." Asked about media reports of his involvement to supply the Contras, Bush countered: "There is this insidious suggestion that I was conducting an operation. It's untrue, unfair, and totally wrong. I met with Max Gomez [Rodriguez's alias] three times and never discussed Nicaragua with him.... There was no linkage to any operation, yet it keeps coming up. There are all kinds of weirdos coming out of the woodwork on this thing." Bush was asked whether or not Donald Gregg "lied" when he denied discussing the Contras with Rodriguez. Bush said no, and that Gregg merely "forgot." "He's not a liar. If I thought he ws a liar, he wouldn't be working for me," the then-Vice President added.

When asked if "in retrospect, do you wish Mr. Gregg had told you about it [North's role in the resupply effort] in August 1986," Bush remarked: "Yes, particularly knowing what I know now."

Which means Gregg must be a liar because he didn't tell the Vice President everything in August 1986, or in April 1986 when Rodriguez complained to him about the profits being skimmed. Yet Bush wasn't at all angry at his chief aide for hiding important information from him, and instead of punishing him, appointed him ambassador to South Korea.

In his autobiography, *Looking Forward* (1987), Bush denies knowing about North's "secret operations" before November 1986.

In a 1988 interview with *Newsweek*, when Bush was asked, "When did you first learn of North's role in the Contra operation?" he answered, "What I know of Mr. North's role in the Contra-resupply effort has come from the information made public during the investigations."

Bush is asking us to believe that he chaired the Task Force on Combating Terrorism, which served as a springboard for North's activities, and the Committee on Crisis Pre-Planning and the National Security Planning Group, but knew nothing of North's activities. He is asking us to believe that Oliver North ran the entire resupply operation on his own, without the knowledge of any of his superiors, as a rogue operation, and when brought to trial merely tried to drag these other men's names and reputations through the mud without grounds. That he only learned of Oliver North's role in the entire Contra-resupply effort from information made public during the investigations. In other words, the Vice President of the United States had no more knowledge or intelligence about Oliver North's secret agendas and covert operations than any average American receiving his news from ABC, *Time*, *Newsweek* and and NBC?

In what must be the ultimate hypocrisy, during the election campaign of 1988 Bush said that the whole issue of Iran-Contra was "old news." "You get sick and tired of saying, I've told the truth."

What became of the Contra connection after Iran-Contra became public? One covert operation which the Bush White House was in all likelihood behind is the secret effort to fund the 1990 campaign of Violeta Chamorro and the National Opposition Union (UNO), the main opposition to the Sandinista candidate, President Daniel Ortega.

In the eight months before the February 25th, 1990, vote, the CIA managed a covert operation which sent more than $600,000 to more than a 100 Miami-based Contra leaders so they could return to Nicaragua (*Newsweek*, October 21st, 1991). Although Congress approved $9 million to be spent on the Nicaraguan election, it banned covert CIA financial support for the UNO.

When asked about the payments, Administration officials claimed the payments were simply expenses for helping 100 or so Contra leaders return home. However, one White House official acknowledged, "We were spending this money for them to go back and work in the Chamorro cam-

paign. They knew what they were supposed to do"
(*Newsweek,* October 21st, 1991).

The payments may have been a continuation
of the money supplied to Contra leaders throughout the 1980s as part of the White House's plan
to destabilize Nicaragua. To do this, the CIA created a Nicaraguan Exile Relocation Program
(NERP), which dispensed the money between July
1989 and February 1990.

Bush and Noriega: How Well Did They Know Each Other?

The extent of George Bush's ties to former Panamanian dictator Manuel Noriega are important
in order to determine what the President knew of
the secret operation to arm the Contras and
whether Contra leaders received money or helped
narcotics traffickers import drugs into the U.S.

Panama General Manuel Noriega's ties to the
U.S. intelligence service go back to 1960, when
as a young cadet at the Peruvian military academy he provided information on leftist students
to the Defense Intelligence Agency.

When Bush became head of the CIA in 1976,
he thwarted an army investigation into Noriega's
activities, code-named "Canton Song", because
he feared it would further damage an already dis-

credited CIA. Noriega, then Panama's chief of intelligence, was buying reel-to-reel audiotapes from the Army's 470th Military Intelligence Group. When Noriega discovered a U.S. wiretap operation against Panamanian officials involved in Canal Treaty negotiations, he bought copies of the tapes for his boss, Ómar Torrijos. Instead of prosecuting Noriega, as the head of the National Security Agency wished, Bush not only didn't punish either him or the officers, he decided to continue paying Noriega an annual sum of $110,000 for his work on behalf of the agency (Frederick Kempe, *Divorcing the Dictator*, Putnam's, as quoted in *Newsweek*, November 15th, 1990).

Bush met Noriega in Washington in December 1976. He denied it at first, then acknowledged the meeting took place, but, in what has become somewhat of a George Bush trademark, remembers nothing of what transpired. Other guests at the lunch say it was the third meeting between the two since Bush became CIA director.

Although CIA Director (under Jimmy Carter) Stansfield Turner had taken Noriega off the payroll of the CIA, by 1981 he was back on.

In December 1983 Bush flew to Panama to meet with Noriega. A Bush spokesperson claims the meeting was a "privileged" talk (whatever that means). Bush told reporters: "What I talked to the

Panamanians about was doing what they could to get their banks out of laundering money for the narcotics traffic" (*Washington Post*, May 8th, 1988). Former U.S. ambassador to Panama Everett Briggs, who also attended the meeting, said that Bush may have sought diplomatic support (for the Contras) but never requested military help. (Of all possible countries, why would the U.S. need to solicit diplomatic support from Panama?) (*Newsweek*, January 15th, 1990). Noriega interpreted this visit as an appeal for help in arming and training the Contras.

José Blandón, a former Panamanian diplomat who was Noriega's top political aide, testified before a Senate investigating committee in February 1988. He says of the same meeting that both Gregg and Bush asked for and got Noriega's commitment to "help secretly arm, train and finance the Contras, which was to begin in early 1984." Gregg denied the meeting ever took place (*Newsweek*, October 31st, 1988).

Further proof of Bush's knowledge of Noriega's support for the Contras was presented at Oliver North's trial in 1989, where it was revealed that a Southern Front Resistance leader had "received $100,000 from Panamanian Defense Forces Chief Noriega in July 1984." Bush, it was claimed, received copies of these documents, which showed Noriega's financial assistance for the Contras (*Newsweek*, January 15th, 1990).

Bush has always pleaded ignorance about Noriega's drug- dealing activities. Yet many of the operatives in Black Eagle, one of the Contra resupply operations Bush and Casey devised in 1982, claim that Noriega played a major role in the operation by providing his country's airfields and front companies, as well as allowing Contras to be trained in Panama. In return, he was given the green light to smuggle cocaine and marijuana into the U.S. on behalf of the Colombian cocaine cartel. According to one retired covert operative, one percent of the gross income generated by th drug traffic was set aside to buy additional weapons for the Contras.

Blandón confirms that the CIA and North used Noriega to funnel guns and money to the Contras, and Panama as a training base. He also claims that Noriega's right-hand man, Mike Harari, told him that Casey and Bush were involved in these operations. "Harari told Noriega in front of me that Bush was very grateful for the help Noriega was providing," Blandón testified.

An Argentine arms dealer who was brought into the operation by Noriega, Jorge Krupnik, told Blandón that everything in the operation had the full backing of Bush and Gregg, including the drug trafficking. Gregg denies meeting Harari or being involved with him (*Newsweek*, January 15th, 1990). Noriega meanwhile gathered a dossier on the role of Bush in the operation, which he referred to when he told a former aide, Colonel Roberto Díaz Herrera, "I've got Bush by the balls," and that he knew things that "could affect the elections of the U.S."

Although Blandón was very credible, there was an immediate attempt by the CIA and Defense Department to discredit him, calling him an "untrustworthy leftist."

"Blandón was the first guy who wasn't a sleazeball who offered evidence against Noriega," says a former Senate Foreign Relations Committee staffer. "He was able to corroborate the testimony we'd been getting from convicted drug dealers, but more important, he was able to put it into a larger context" (*New York*, January 15th, 1990).

It's not as if the administration never realized or discovered what was happening. They tried to block any investigation which might implicate U.S. government officials in any way with Noriega's drug trafficking. Blandón testified that the White House knew Noriega was involved in drug trafficking since the early days of the Administration, but because of the support Noriega gave the Contras, ignored it.

In the spring of 1988, when the General Accounting Office (GAO), the investigative branch of Congress, opened an investigation, using Panama as a case study of how drug trafficking by foreign officials influences U.S. foreign policy decisions, the White House ordered the State Department, the Pentagon, the CIA and the Drug Enforcement Administration not to cooperate. According to a UPI report on August 18th, 1988, on the stonewall effort, "Democrats and investigators said the White House order was aimed at preventing potentially embarrassing discoveries from rocking the presidential campaign of Republican Vice President George Bush." In August 1988 the White House said that the Justice Department had decided that "the subject matter of the request is beyond the GAO's statutory authority" (*Common Cause*, September/October 1988).

The report might very well have revealed George Bush's knowledge of the United States' ties with Noriega. Yet the White House, specifically the National Security Council (NSC), intervened. GAO investigators discovered that officials of the State Department, Justice Department, Customs Service and Drug Enforcement Agency were told they couldn't assist the probe until the NSC agreed (*Washington Post*, March 12th, 1989). According to a chronology of one of the GAO investigators, the State and Justice officials were instructed by the NSC "not to deal with us until [the] NSC had developed operational guidelines on what to do and what not to do on this assignment" *(Washington Post*, March 21st, 1989).

Nancy Kingsbury, who at that time was a senior official in the GAP's National Security and International Affairs Divison, commented on the NSC's coordinating activities, "The NSC would not ordinarily have played that kind of role" (*Washington Post*, March 21st, 1989).

The White House effort to protect Noriega may also been because of the useful role the Panamanian dictator played in the Reagan-Bush Administration's Central American foreign policy. One former national security assistant to President Ronald Reagan claims the U.S. government "conspired" for years to protect Panamanian General Manuel Noriega and "willfully ignored" evidence of his narcotics activities because he had agreed to help the Contras.

Norman Bailey, who served as a director of planning on the National Security Counsel staff and was a former special assistant to President Reagan for national security affairs, doesn't believe Reagan Administration officials when they say they didn't have enough solid evidence of Noriega's narcotics activities to indict him in February 1988, more than eighteen months before President Bush sent U.S. troops into Panama to oust and arrest him.

In September 1988, Admiral Daniel Murphy, Bush's top drug aide, declared: "I never saw any intelligence suggesting General Noriega's involvement in the drug trade. In fact, we always held up Panama as the model in terms of cooperation with the United States in the war on drugs" (*Convergence*, Christic Institute, Fall 1991).

Bailey disagrees. Testifying before the House Select Committee on Narcotics Abuse and Control in March 1988, he said, "Black and white evidence about Noriega's narcotics activities has been available since at least the mid-1970s. It could have been read by any authorized official of the U.S. government with appropriate security clearances" (*Common Cause*, September/October 1988).

The question is: To what extent was the Reagan-Bush Administration's policy on drug trafficking influenced by the help they were getting from people like Noriega?

Senator Kerry says the congressional hearings he chaired showed that "stopping drug trafficking to the U.S. has been a secondary U.S. foreign policy objective. It has been sacrificed repeatedly for other political goals" (*Common Cause*, September/October 1988).

Francis McNeil, a former senior Deputy Assistant Secretary of State for intelligence and research, told the Senate in April 1988 that "some government officials looked away when they thought vigorous pursuit of narcotics trafficking conflicted with national security priorities."

Another question which arises is: Because of the Administration's commitment to the Contra effort, and due to the ties Contra supporters had with narcotics traffickers, was the White House's commitment to keeping dangerous drugs out of the U.S. compromised?

As Vice President, George Bush headed two main administration initiatives to coordinate drug investigations: the South Florida Task Force and the National Narcotics Border Interdiction System (NNBIS). Despite their being created as a clearinghouse for intelligence, former DEA Administrator Francis Mullen and the GAO criticized the two groups for not doing that, but instead establishing an intelligence network which bypassed DEA contacts and "threatened to fragment the narcotics intelligence database."

In 1987 the GAO said of NNBIS: "Seizures are small compared to the amounts of drugs successfully smuggled into the U.S."

Mullen claimed that these two groups were inflating drug-seizures statistics and that the public was being misled about the two organizatons' successes. "If NNBIS continues unchecked it will discredit other federal drug programs and become the adminstration's Achilles heel for drug law enforcement," he warned.

Supporting the Contras also blinded other moral fibers of the Reagan-Bush White House. In 1984, Honduran General José Buesco, a supporter of the Contras, was labeled by the Justice Department as an international terrorist, and was indicted in connection with a plot to kill President of Honduras Roberto Suazo Córdova, which was to be financed with profits from cocaine smuggling.

Senior administration officials, including Oliver North, Assistant Secretary of State Elliot Abrams, and former National Security Advisor John Poindexter, tried to get leniency for Buesco due to his role in helping set up Contra camps on Honduras' border with Nicaragua. When the plot to kill Suazo Córdova was discovered, Buesco agreed to come to the U.S. to face charges, but officials from the Department of Defense and the CIA started asking for leniency, a full pardon, sentence reduction or deportation. On September 17th, 1986, North sent a message to Poindexter stating that the administration should help Buesco because if not, "he will break his longstanding silence about the Nicaraguan resistance and other sensitive operations."

The Justice Department, particularly Deputy Assistant Attorney General Mark Richard, opposed leniency for Buesco. Richard would later testify to the Iran-Contra Committee that Abrams insisted "we should do what we can to accommodate this man." The Justice Department still refused, and Buesco eventually pleaded guilty to two felony charges in the attempted assassination plot and was sentenced to two five-year jail terms.

McNeil believes that it wasn't only Buesco's support for the Contras that encouraged the Administration to help him, but also what North told Poindexter in a memo was "songs nobody wants to hear."

Hoping perhaps that George Bush was listening at the time, McNeil told the Senate subcommittee: "We're certainly going to have to stop giving these signals that if you have a military or intelligence relationship with the U.S., it's a license to commit major crimes in this country."

Conclusion

How did Bush get away with it?

For starters, disinformation became a very powerful and influential tool in the Reagan years, particularly when it was used against an unknowing public.

A major part of this disinformation effort was to manipulate the public with the "kick ass" image of the Reagan-Bush White House. With the use of key phrases such as "counter-terrorism," "anti-terrorism," "the war on terrorism," and "the

Russians are behind all acts of international terrorism," the Reagan Administration was seen as a group of highly committed, morally upstanding national leaders and gained the confidence of the American public. This reservoir of public goodwill the Administration created stood up well to allegations made against Reagan's or Bush's knowledge of involvement in Iran-Contra. When Irangate first broke, most Americans really didn't think the President knew because it was difficult to conceive of Ronald Reagan lying about anything. With the entire question being whether Reagan did or did not know of the diversion of profits from arms sales to Iran to buy arms for the Contras, Bush was let off the hook.

The question of George Bush's guilt in Iran-Contra comes down to two possibilities: either he knew everything, or, while all the efforts to resupply the Contras were happening, he was kept in the dark by Gregg and was absent from all meetings where arms-for-hostages were discussed.

Could it be that Gregg knew everything but kept it from the Vice President? That despite all the committees which bore the Vice President's name, he didn't attend the meetings and had no interest in or knowledge of what policies were implemented there?

Could it be that a lone Lt. Colonel in the National Security Council could carry out an entire private foreign policy by arming and financing the Contras without anyone in the White House knowing about it or finding out? And if so, and the Vice Prsident or his National Security Advisor didn't discover these activities, what does that say about their level of competence?

Of course George Bush knew everything. How could he not have known?

In fact, far from being a wimp, George Bush ran the White House. Says former Army investigator Gene Wheaton: "Ronald Reagan may have been President but George Bush was in charge. Weinberger and Schultz were no match for a covert operator like him."

Bush was smart. He figured out that to implement his secret agendas all he had to do was arrange it so he was appointed chairman of all the important White House committees: the President's Task Force on Narcotics, Terrorism, Deregulation of the Savings and Loans and Airlines Industry. This meant he could appoint the key people to work on these inter-agency committees to establish policy and Bush's covert agendas.

The scary part of all this is that Bush seemed to be invincible. No one could pin him down and corner him by saying: "Of course you know about these secret agendas and covert operations. You were there. Stop treating us like a bunch of imbeciles and explain to us how with these covert operations going on all around you, you, the Vice President, didn't know about them?"

No one did that. Not Congress. Not the press. Nor any of the presidential contenders in 1988 and 1992. Like any good covert operator, Bush has a brilliant cover. About the only thing the American people knew about this President is that he joggs, fishes, and has a dog.

They called Reagan the Teflon President. Bush has him beat by a mile.

Vice President Quayle's Role In President Bush's CIA Agenda

When Dan Quayle was chosen as George Bush's vice-presidential candidate most people had never heard of him. Some speculated that he was "impeachment insurance" for Bush in case Iran-Contra blew up in his face if he was elected President. Others claimed that it was to satisfy the conservative wing of the Republican Party.

While the media labeled Quayle as an "idiot" and the public views him as a dummy, incapable of sophisticated thinking, Bush knew otherwise. He chose Quayle because of the ability of Quayle to carry out covert operations, such as the key role he played in the secret effort to supply the Contras during the Reagan White House.

To carry out his secret agendas Bush has to control key committees in the House and Senate, such as Finance, Intelligence, and Armed Forces, and command the loyalty of legislative assistants to congressmen and senators. Senator Quayle served the then-Vice President Bush well in the Senate as an integral part of the Secret Team. He was the Vice President's point man for the Contras, soothing Congress' mind over the nasty rumors it was hearing about the Contras' ties to drug dealers and unscrupulous mercenary groups. When money is spent, congressmen and senators have to be informed. When "humanitarian aid" for the Contras was granted by Congress, Quayle did the explaining.

In the summer of 1991 I got to know William Northrup, the Israeli arms dealer who was arrested in Bermuda in 1986 for selling arms to Iran. Before leaving for the States in September, he told me to try and get out to California and meet Gene Wheaton. "Gene's a good man," he assured me.

Wheaton had been investigating Reagan-Bush covert operations since the early 1980s and had seen from the inside how these secret agendas operated. In addition to his 25 years' experience as a criminal investigator for the U.S. Army, he had designed security systems for airports in the Middle East and served as an anti-smuggling narcotics advisor to the Shah.

By that time I had interviewed covert operators like Richard Secord, and Iran-Contra players such as Yaacov Nimrodi. Now I had someone who looked at the world of covert operations from the perspective of an investigator. Unlike intelligence agents, Wheaton didn't thrive on lies and deceit. Judging from his very modest home, he obviously wasn't in it for the money.

In 1985 Wheaton was vice president of a small cargo airline company that Oliver North's network wanted to use to haul arms to the Contras and rebels elsewhere, such as in Afghanistan. Wheaton had the expertise the secret team wanted, so they set out to recruit him. While Wheaton may have fit their political profile, he was conservative and right-wing; he was a cop, not an intelligence agent. He was brought into the center circle, where he stayed long enough to learn about the White House's ties to drug runners, the massive arms transfers to rebel groups, the mountains of falsified documentation and miscarriages of justice.

"I had no objection to the covert end of it, as long as it was legal," says Wheaton. "It wasn't. Whenever I asked about the legality of certain operation I was told, "It's all right, this is a vital national security issue.' I talked myself out of the inner circle but I was in it long enough to get to know the players and their method of operation. The government officials I met in the Pentagon called supporting the private covert operator 'in-

telligence support activity.' These covert operators trampled on our Constitution and made a
mockery of our judicial system. They aren't moti-
vated strictly by anti-communism, power, or
money, but by the adrenaline that stems from being able to create chaos. They would gladly destabilize a democratic ally of America just so they
can go back in and save it."

Wheaton explains that the origins of Oliver
North's network was in the mid-1970s. There
were, he says, literally tens of thousands of
ex-covert operators and former Air America "employees" running around loose in the U.S. These
weren't the kind of guys to lay back and run 7-11
stores, so they set up an array of covert airlines
using the assets of Air America, the former CIA
proprietary airline which had helped fly heroin
out of Burma and Laos.

When Air America was liquidated it created
scores of smaller airlines, including Global, Capital, and Southern Cross. All tolled, these companies employed over 15,000 people. The subsidiary companies of Air America, Southern Air
Transport, Continental Air Services, and Air Asia
were also broken up. This meant this secret team
was able to supply pilots and mechanics, logistics and control people for future, privatized covert operations.

The 800 or so covert operators who got thrown

out of the CIA by Jimmy Carter in 1977 allied themselves with the conservative element of the Republican Party. Their goal was to get George Bush elected to either president or Vice President. They didn't care which one it was, as long as their man got into the White House. They rallied around Bush and worked like a political action committee. They put their unique talents into action. They were going to do in America what they had done throughout the 1960s and 1970s in Africa and South and Central America: rig elections and overthrow governments.

One aspect of the covert operators' activities was the "October Surprise" theory, which claims members of Reagan's 1980 campaign team, including George Bush and William Casey, made a deal with Iranian leaders not to release the 52 American hostages they were holding until after the November presidential election.

Wheaton claims Quayle was brought "into the game," Bush and Casey's network of the Secret Team, early on. He believes that a major source of Quayle's political power in his home state of Indiana comes from an old friend of William Casey's, Beurt SerVaas, who was on the executive board of the Veterans of the OSS, the predecessor organization of the CIA. SerVaas's daughter is married to what Wheaton describes as an "off-the-books" French intelligence asset, Bernard

Marie. Wheaton says that he introduced Marie to Defense Intelligence Agency officials who were part of the Reagan-Bush White House's secret arms deals with Iran in the early 1980s.

"Quayle is being groomed," says Wheaton. "Quayle was a true believer and they wanted to bring him up through the ranks. It wasn't easy for Bush and Casey to find people who would go along with their far right-wing philosophy, who at the same time were articulate and presentable." Quayle's "smoking gun" was Robert Owen and Owen's ties were to John Hull, a native of Indiana who owned and managed 8000 acres of land in northern Costa Rica 30 miles from the Nicaraguan border. The CIA and Oliver North used Hull's ranch as a supply depot to move weapons to the Contras. Hull used American government protection to fly drugs from there into the U.S., sometimes on the very same planes.

Over the next few years, four companies which were also used by Hull to smuggle Colombian cocaine to the U.S. from his ranch, received more than $800,000 of State Department funds under this program. Frigorificos de Puntareñas, a Costa Rican shrimp company, had cocaine shipped from Hull's ranch to Costa Rican ports packed in frozen shrimp and delivered to Miami and Guf ports (*Out of Control*, page 157). In February 1986 Oliver North chose Vortex Aircraft Sales and

Leasing to fly the so-called humanitarian assistance to the Contras. At the same time, that company's vice president, Michael Palmer, a fomer Delta Airlines pilot turned drug smuggler, was under indictment for marijuana trafficking (*The Nation*, August 29th, 1987).

Other companies which received Contra "humanitarian aid" included Setco, which was controlled by a billionaire drug lord currently serving a life sentence in a Federal prison for the torture-murder of a Drug Enforcement Agency agent. According to an FBI report, another company, Diacsa, served as a central distribution point for cocaine trafficking and money laundering (Senate Foreign Relations Subcommittee on Narcotics, Terrorism and International Organizations, April 1989).

Owen's ties to Calero are confirmed by Joseph Adams, a former Marine Corps intelligence officer, who trained with the elite Delta Force unit of the U.S. Army. Adams was the security chief and consultant to Calero from the fall of 1984 to the spring of 1986. He lead a team of American mercenaries and a Pentagon intelligence agent on a two-month combat mission inside Nicaragua called "Operation Pegasus."

Adams says that Calero met Owen on a number of occasions. "Rob Owen was Adolfo's contact," Adams says. "I met with Owen several times with Adolfo. Rob was reporting to Adolfo on the Southern Front activities." Adams remembers at least a dozen such meetings in 1984 and 1985 (*The Progressive*, March 1987).

While being interviewed by the CBS News program *West 57th St.*, Jack Terrel, a military commander for a private American group that supplied trainers for the Contras and who was a key witness for Senator Kerry's Senate investigation of the Contras' ties to drug trafficking, said he met twice with John Hull and Robert Owen and that Owen was the go-between between Costa Rica and the White House, and the "bag man" for Oliver North.

Said Terrel: "Owen told me, "I take a $10,000 a month to John Hull from the National Security Council for these types of operations, and, if we need more money, that's no problem' " (*West 57th St.*, June 25th, 1986). When John Hull was asked by CBS News if he knew Owen, he replied: "I've met Rob on several occasions. I have no business dealings with Rob." When asked what he did for living, Hull said; "I have no idea."

Mike Wallace of CBS News asked Terrel if he had ever heard about Hull's drug smuggling, to which Terrel answered, "We've got a cancer here; it's like Watergate. It's not going away."

U.S. investigative bodies were simply not interested in hearing about John Hull's deeds. "We sent stuff to all the committees," says Tony Avrigan, who together with his wife and fellow journalist Martha Honey, filed suit along with the Christic Institute in a Federal court in Miami charging Calero and officials in the American government with planning the May 30th, 1984, La Penca, Nicaragua, bombing at a press conference held by Contra leader Eden Pastora. "We made everything available to them" (*The Progressive*, March 1990).

The Iran-Contra investigating committees sent Thomas Polgar, a former CIA station chief in Vietnam, to Costa Rica to investigate charges that Hull was involved in drug dealing. He too wasn't too interested in getting at the truth. "Polgar didn't want to hear anything specific¾dates, evidence, sources," said Beth Hawkins, a journalist who worked for the *Tico Times*, in San José. "His questions were subjective, what we thought about Pastora and Hull" (*The Progressive*, March 1990).

Avrigan remarks on the difference between the U.S. government's treatment of John Hull and that of Manuel Noriega in its efforts to bring drug dealers to justice. "It just shows very clearly that in the eyes of the United States, Noriega only became a drug dealer when he stopped taking orders from the CIA. Drug traffickers who continue to take orders from the CIA are protected" (*The Progressive*, March 1990).

There is also ample proof that the U.S. government not only rejected allegations of Contra involvement in drug tracking, but also tipped off these smugglers when they had become targets of an investigation.

Journalist Jonathan Kwitny says Hull acknowledged to him that he was warned in early 1985 by a NSC source of a potential investigation. After discussing the matter with the U.S. Embassy in Costa Rica, he declined to talk with Justice Department officials (*The Nation*, August 29th, 1987). Kwitny investigated other charges that the NSC tipped off drug dealers of pending investigations. He says an American filmmaker, Lawrence Spivy, who in early 1985 had worked with the Contra supply operation, saw FBI memos from Miami about North's Office ties to drug smugglers.

The U.S. government not only tolerated drug dealers like Hull and informed them of any investigation of their activities, they also assisted them by intervening on their behalf when they got caught.

Costa Rican prosecutor Jorge Chavarria Guzmán had unsuccessfuly tried to charge Hull for his role in the 1984 La Penca bombing. Guzmán claims that Robert Owen had foreknowledge of the bombing.

When Hull eventually was arrested for drug

trafficking, the U.S. Embassy in Costa Rica, officials of the Bush Administration, and no less than 19 legislators petitioned Costa Rican President Oscar Arias to have him released (*The Progressive*, April 1989).

In a January 26th, 1989, letter, Lee Hamilton, co-chairman of the House committee that investigated the Iran-Contra scandals, wrote, "It is our hope that Mr. Hull's case will be concluded promptly and that it will be handled in a manner that will not complicate U.S.-Costa Rican relations. We understand that his arrest occurred under unusual circumstances. We urge you to investigate Mr. Hull's case to ensure that the charges against him have been brought with just cause and to ensure that his rights under Costa Rican law and under the Universal Declaration of Human Rights are protected" (*The Progressive*, March 1990).

President Arias wrote Hamilton back, reminding him that it was up to the courts, not himself, to judge Hull's case. "It pains me," he responded, "that you insinuate that the exemplary relations between your country and mine could deteriorate because our legal system is fighting against drug trafficking, no matter how powerful the people who participate in it, or what external backing they might have" (*The Progressive*, March 1990).

Hull jumped bail in August 1989 and fled to

the United States. He charged that the murder allegations were because the "the government down there [Costa Rica] is infiltrated and manipulated by communists headed up by the Christic Institute" (*The Progressive*, March 1990).

It may be difficult for most people to comprehend that the American government employs drug dealers in its foreign policy pursuits. Yet unless everyone in this story is lying in order to defame the White House, or John Hull, or Robert Owen, then this is exactly what happened.

Quayle could argue that he knew nothing of this because it began after Owen left the position as his legislative assistant. Yet the question remains: Why was Owen chosen for the task in the first place? At least in 1983, Owen, when he was still working for Quayle, knew Hull, and introduced him around Washington on behalf of Quayle's Office to key senators and congressional supporters of the Contras. Did Owen know then that Hull was involved in CIA run drugs? Did Quayle?

George Bush and the Secret Team of Covert Operators

Was The Reagan-Bush White House In Cahoots With Drug Lords?

Did the Reagan-Bush White House do business with drug traffickers? This question not only applies to the Presidencies of George Bush and Ronald Reagan, but to every single administration since the end of World War II.

The Christic Institute and its founder, Daniel Sheehan, deserve special credit for its work in exposing the CIA's ties to drug lords, particularly during the Reagan years. Founded in 1980 as a non-profit, public-interest law firm and public policy center, the Christic Institute had previously prosecuted some of the most celebrated public-interest lawsuits of the decade, including the Karen Silkwood case and the Greensboro Massacre suit against the American Nazi Party and Ku Klux Klan.

During one of my trips to Washington I finally got a chance to meet Sheehan. Although situated only a few blocks from Washington's Union Station, it seemed only right that a non-profit organization fighting against the tremendous odds in facing covert operators would be housed in a run-down, near-slum neighborhood of the nation's capital.

Although we had just a short time together because I was flying back to Israel that evening, Sheehan struck me as being one of the very few people in the United States who grasped most of the complexities of the story of how the CIA had become involved with drug traffickers. The way he rattled off the names and events, he could probably have repeated them in his sleep.

Sheehan claims that there existed a conspiratorial "secret team" of covert operators which carried out its own, private foreign policy much of it funded by proceeds from the international drug trade. The 29 defendants named in a suit instituted by the Christic Institute in Florida included Lt. Colonel Oliver North, retired major generals

Richard Secord and John Singlaub, former CIA intelligence officers Theodore Shackley and Thomas Clines, financier Albert Hakim, Robert Owen, a former aide to Vice President Quayle, Contra rebel leader Adolfo Calero, mercenary Thomas Posey, and drug dealers John Hall and Jorge Ochoa.

"We assembled evidence that the Contra resupply network orchestrated criminal covert operations, including secret wars, assassination programs and illicit arms deals. It financed these activities, in part, through the smuggling and sale of tons of cocaine and other illegal drugs into the United States," says Sheehan. "Since the Congress, the Reagan-Bush White House's Justice Department, and the Judiciary had, for the most part, turned a blind eye to these allegations, we took our evidence directly to the American public. The public needs to know and has a right to know of covert and illegal activities undertaken by private citizens in the name of U.S. foreign policy and 'national security.' "

In the lawsuit, the institute used the RICO statutes, passed in 1970 to bring Mafia bosses to justice (the statutes enable a member of a conspiracy to be held accountable for crimes committed by those under his orders). The institute was able to formally charge the Reagan-Bush Secret Team as a result of the 1984 bombing of a press conference in La Penca, Nicaragua. During the early part of 1984, after the Boland Amendments were passed, Oliver North came up with a new plan to secretly circumvent the congressional ban on Contra military aid. The idea was to take away the responsibility of arming and training them from the CIA and transfer it to a "private" network controlled directly by him from the White House. This meant uniting the various Contra forces into one effective fighting force.

One of the Contra leaders, Eden Pastora of the ARDE organization based in Costa Rica, refused a CIA ultimatum to ally his group with the larger Contra force the administration was supporting, the FDN. He was told by the CIA to "unite with the FDN or suffer the consequences."

At a press conference where Pastora was to announce that he was not going to accede to these demands, a bomb exploded, killing eight people and injuring many others. The White House obviously wouldn't take no for an answer.

Sheehan alleges that the explosion was arranged by Hull, a drug trafficker who helped Oliver North's Contra supply operation, and Felipe Vidal, another narcotics smuggler who worked with Hull. At a crucial December 1984 meeting at the Shamrock Hilton Hotel in Houston, Texas, attended by Hull and Owen, Jack Terrell, another participant in North's supply network, claims that Hull told him "Pastora had to be killed" (*The Progressive*, March 1990).

The CIA helped cover up the bombing through extensive use of disinformation within Costa Rica. A Costa Rican government report revealed that in 1984 CIA agent Dimitrius Papas trained an elite 15-member group of Costa Rican intelligence agents known as "the Babies" to organize a network of illegal telephone taps and a slush fund for payoffs to Costa Rican leaders (*The Progressive*, March 1990; *Newsweek*, February 12th, 1990).

During the course of preparing for the suit, Sheehan met Paul Hoven, a Vietnam veteran who led a group called "Project on Military Procurement" in support of military reform in the purchasing and development of weapons (*Out of Control: The Story of the Reagan Administration's Secret War in Nicaragua, the Illegal Arms Pipeline, and the Contra Drug Connection*, 1987). Hoven introduced Sheehan to a retired military intelligence officer who had first hand knowledge about a group of former CIA senior officials who formed a "secret team" to undertake covert operations on a commercial basis. Operating independently of the U.S. government, some members were even involved in CIA-sanctioned assassination plots as far back as the Kennedy era. The former intelligence officer told

Sheehan he came in contct with the secret team when he tried to acquire semi-covert mercenary work in Central America and Iran.

This convinced Sheehan that a secret team did exist and that his institute had do something to stop them.

He knew who the criminals were. When he found his victims, two American journalists based in Costa Rica, Tony Avigran and Martha Honey, who were injured in the blast, he set the legal work in motion. The institute's lawsuit was filed on May 29th, 1986, in the U.S. District Court of Southern Florida. The racketeering charges described a complex criminal enterprise, including former United States military and intelligence officers, mercenaries, businessmen, and drug dealers, who conspired to covertly organize military aid to the Contra forces. The Court Declaration charted the racketeering activities from 1959 through 1987, and divided them into geographical locations: Cuba, Southeast Asia, Iran, Afghanistan, and Nicaragua.

Cuba

In Cuba, Sheehan's account of the Secret Team's activities begins in the late 1950s and early 1960s with a plan to overthrow Cuban dictator Fidel

Castro, which violated the United States' Neutrality Act. Expatriate Cubans were recruited and sent to one of two secret military training bases established for this purpose¾one in the south of Miami, Florida, and the other, named Camp Trax, in Retalhuleu, Guatemala (*Inside the Shadow Government*, 1988).

The force later became known as the 2506 Brigade. The purpose of their missions was to allow the expatriate Cubans to re-enter Cuba covertly and establish a center of guerrilla resistance to the Cuban government and to disrupt the new economy. A later plan included the assassination of Fidel Castro (*Report of the Select Committee to Study Governmental Operations with Respect to Intelligence Activities, Alleged Assassination Plots Involving Foreign Leaders*, 94th Congress, 1975). This would have paved the way for former President Fulgencio Batista's return to power as well as the narcotics and gambling activities run by such underworld figures as Meyer Lansky and Santo Trafficante, Jr.

The low-profile, guerrilla-infiltration assassination strategy, code-named Operation 40, was replaced with a plan for a full-scale military invasion of Cuba, to be staged at the Bay of Pigs in April 1962. After that invasion failed, from 1962 to 1965 Theodore Shackley headed a program of raids and sabotage against Cuba. Working under

Shackley was Thomas Clines, Rafael Quintero, Luis Posada Carriles, Rafaël and Raúl Villaverde, Frank Sturgis (who would later be one of the famous Watergate burglars), Felix Rodriguez and Edwin Wilson. This operation, called JM/WAVE, was eventually closed down in 1965, when several of its participants became involved with smuggling narcotics from Cuba into the United States (*New York Times*, January 4th, 1975).

Southeast Asia

When the JM/WAVE project ended, Shackley and Clines, Rodriguez, Wilson, and Quintero left for Laos in Southeast Asia. Shackley was chief of the CIA's station in Vientiane until 1969, while Clines was under Shackley's direction as the base chief in Long Tieng. (*The Ravens: The Men Who Flew in Aerica's Secret War in Laos*, 1987)

The goal of these two covert operators was to organize, direct, and fund an army of Hmong tribesmen (historically, opium poppy farmers) on bases in northern Laos to fight the Communist Pathet Lao insurgent forces. The leader of this secret army was general Vang Pao, who was also a major opium supplier. In 1960 a civil war broke out when General Phoumi Nosavan's right-wing government was overthrown by a group of army officers, together with former Prime Minister Souvanna Phouma and leftist leader Pathet Lao. Nosavan recruited Pao to take control over northeastern Laos with Shackley and Clines providing air support. In return for fighting the Communists, Shackley, Clines and Richard Secord helped Pao control Laos' opium trade by sabotaging competitors. Secord oversaw and authorized the transport of raw opium by Pao's tribesmen in paramilitary aircraft from the mountain opium fields to processing centers. Eventually, Vang Pao had a monopoly over the heroin trade in Laos (*Inside the Shadow Government*).

Six air bases were built in Thailand and Long Tieng in northern Laos as well as landing strips for Air America planes throughout Hmong--controlled territory (David Truong, *Running Drugs and Secret Wars*, *Covert Action* Information Bulletin No. 28, Summer 1987). In 1967 Shackley and Clines helped Vang Pao attain financial backing to form his own airline, Zieng Khouang Air Transport Co., to transport opium and heroin between Long Tieng and Vientiane. In 1968, Shackley and Clines arranged a meeting in Saigon between Mafia chief Santo Trafficante, Jr., and Vang Pao to establish a heroin-smuggling operation from Southeast Asia to the United States (*The Politics of Heroin*, 1972).

Ron Rickenbach was a former official with the

U.S Agency for International Development who served in Laos from 1962 to 1969. "Early on," he wrote, "I think that we all believed that what we were doing was in the best interest of America, that we were in fact perhaps involved in some not so desirable aspects of the drug traffic, however we believed strongly in the beginning that we were there for a just cause. These people were willing to take up arms. We needed to stop the Red threat" (PBS documentary "*Frontline: "Guns, Drugs and the CIA*," May 1989).

Although Richard Secord claims that "there was no commercial trade in opium going on," Rickenbach says: "I was in the areas where opium was transshipped, I personally was witness to opium being placed on aircraft, American aircraft. I witnessed it being taken off smaller aircraft that were coming in from outlying areas."

Former Air America pilot Neil Hanses adds, "Yes, I've seen the sticky bricks come on board and no one was challenging their right to carry it."

Another smuggling route had the opium being traded for guns before being loaded onto planes operated by the French Corsican drug syndicates and dropped into the Gulf of Siam. It would later be picked up by fishing boats and taken to ports in South Vietnam.

As part of their covert operation, with training

by Quintero and Rodriguez, Vang Pao is reported to have killed rival opium warlords, civilian functionaries, and supporters of the Pathet Lao (*Inside the Shadow Government*). These actions were continuing when in 1969 Clines and Shackley were posted to Saigon, where they are alleged to have directed "Operation Phoenix" to "neutralize" non-combatant Vietnamese civilians suspected of collaborating with the National Liberation Front. Former CIA director William Colby would later testify at a 1971 Senate hearing that "Operation Phoenix" killed 20,587 Vietnamese and imprisoned another 28,978 between August 1968 and May 1971 (Fred Branfman, *South Vietnam's Police and Prison System: The U.S. Connection*, Free Press, 1978).

Alfred McCoy, a professor of history at the University of Wisconsin, wrote the monumental work on the subject of the CIA's involvement in the drug trade: *The Politics of Heroin in SouthEast Asia* . In 1991 he followed it up with *The Politics of Heroin: CIA Complicity in the Global Drug Trade*.

McCoy has specialized in the area of the CIA's historic ties to the international drug trade. He asserts that the organization's involvement in the Asian drug trade actually dates back to the late 1940s, after the People's Republic of China was proclaimed by Mao Tse-tung. The CIA allied itself with Kuomintang forces that had fled to the Shan states of northern Burma to carry out sabotage against China. They supported themselves via the opium trade by sending caravans of the drug to Laos for sale.

"Whenever the CIA supports a rebel faction in a regional dispute, that faction's involvement in the drug trade increases," McCoy claims. "Just as CIA support for National Chinese troops in the Shan states increased Burma's opium crop in the 1950s, so too did the agency's aid to the mujahideen guerrillas in the 1980s expand opium production in Afghanistan" (*The Progressive*, July 1991).

Victor Marchetti, who worked for the CIA for 14 years and served as executive assistant to the deputy director under Richard Helms until 1969, is probably the leading critic today of the CIA's "covert" activities. Having seen how things work from the inside, in 1975 he wrote *The CIA and the Cult of Intelligence*, the first book to expose the workings of the U.S. organization. The book has become somewhat of a classic in certain circles. On April 18th, 1972, Marchetti became the first American writer to be served with an official censorship order issued by a court of the United States forbidding him to disclose any information about the CIA. The verdict was eventually overturned.

"I guess people like the book," Marchetti told me one morning at a coffee shop in the National Press Building in Washington. "Every once in a while I get a royalty check for a few hundred dollars from my publishers."

Marchetti was a Soviet military specialist and at one point was probably the U.S. government's leading expert on Soviet military aid to the countries of the Third World. He left the CIA and wrote about its shortcomings. He felt the agency was incapable of reforming itself and that Presidents had no interest in changing it because they viewed it as a private asset.

Out of all the people I interviewed for this book, Marchetti was perhaps the most insightful. He spoke about covert operations and secret agendas of the Bush-Reagan White Houses the way most people would about yesterday's football scores.

"It shouldn't surprise anyone that the history of the CIA runs parallel to criminal and drug operations throughout the world," he says. "The connection stretches back to the predecessor organization of the CIA, the OSS [Office of Strategic Services], and its involvement with the Italian Mafia, the Cosa Nostra, in Sicily and Southern Italy. When the OSS was fighting communists in France they 'mingled' with the Corsican brotherhood, who were heavily into drugs at that time."

Many of these contacts were formulated in the late 1940's when the OSS worked covertly to replace the leftist leaders of the Marseilles dock union, after it was thought that the union might interfere with American shipping in a crisis (*The Nation*, August 29th, 1987).

Exploiting the drug trade amplifies the operational capacity of covert operations for the CIA. When the CIA decides to enter a region to combat a communist force or country, the purpose is to seek out allies and assets which are effective and won't squeal. The CIA's allies' involvement with narcotics enhances their operational capacity because they are fully integrated into the household economies of the region and monopolize what is usually the largest cash crop in that country. Any group which controls such a lucrative trade commands extraordinary political power that is extremely useful to the CIA. Powerful drug warlords can mobilize people to die. No amount of money in the world can buy this operational capacity.

Says AlfredMcCoy: "In the mountain ranges along the southern rim of Asia¾whether in Afghanistan, Burma, or Laos¾opium is the main currency of external trade and thus is a key source of political power. Since operations involve alliances with local power brokers who serve as the CIA's commanders, the agency, perhaps unwillingly or unwittingly, has repeatedly found its covert operations enmeshed with Asia's heroin trade. By investing a local ally such as Hekmatyar or Vang Pao with the authority of its alliance, the CIA draws the ally under the mantle of its protection. So armed, a tribal leader, now less vulnerable to arrest and prosecution, can use his American alliance to expand his share of the local opium trade" (*The Politics of Heroin*, 1991).

Marchetti agrees: "Drug dealers are in a position to know things, to get things done. They have muscle and no qualms about using it. This is attractive to the covert operators."

Nugan Hand Bank

Covert operations, like any other type of operation, need financing and the use of financial instruments. Just as BCCI served a useful purpose for many countries' and dictators' illicit activities, back in the mid-1970s the Secret Team decided it needed to control its own bank for covert operations.

Daniel Sheehan gathered information which suggests Clines, Secord, Shackley, and Quintero siphoned off a percentage of the funds derived from the opium profits of Vang Pao to a secret bank account at the Nugan Hand Bank in Sydney, Australia.

The Nugan Bank was founded in 1976 by Francis John Nugan and Michael Jon Hand. Hand was a member of the U.S. Special Forces in Laos, a former Green Beret and a CIA agent. Shortly after its establishment the bank boasted deposits of $25 million. Its board of directors was impressive.

The President of the Nugan Hand Bank was Admiral Earl F. Yates, former Chief of Staff for Strategic Planning of U.S. Forces in Asia and the Pacific. The President of Nugan Hand Bank Hawaii was General Edwin F. Black, commander of U.S. troops in Thailand during the Vietnam War and then-Assistant Army Chief of Staff for the Pacific. Nugan Hand's representative in Saudi Arabia was Bernie Houghton, a U.S. Naval Intelligence agent.

Another director of Nugan Hand Bank was Dale Holmgree, a former employee of Civil Air Transport, which later became the CIA's proprietary company, Air America (the airline run by the CIA that transported opium out of the Golden Triangle to Saigon, Hong Kong, and Bangkok). George Farris, a Green Beret and CIA operative in Vietnam, ran the Washington, D.C., office of Nugan Hand Bank. General LeRoy J. Manor, former Chief of Staff for the U.S. Pacific Command, was Nugan Hand's man in Manila. The bank's legal counsel was William Colby, a former director of the CIA.

The Board of Directors for the parent company that preceded the establishment of the Nugan Hand Bank, were Grant Walters, Robert Peterson, David M. Houton, and Spencer Smith, all of whom listed their address as C/O Air America, Army Post Office, San Francisco, California (*Canadian Dimension*, September 1987).

Despite having established branches throughout the world, the Nugan Hand Bank rarely conducted any banking activities. In fact, the bank was a mini-BCCI, its reah spanning six continents, and was involved in drug operations, laundering money, tax evasion, and investor fraud operations. Not only did it serve as a transaction center for the profits the CIA earned from the Southeast Asian drug trade, but it also funneled money to South African-backed forces fighting in Angola.

The bank made the headlines of Australia in 1980 when Frank Nugan was found dead from a gunshot wound in his Mercedes-Benz on January 27th of that year. In his trousers police found the business card of Nugan Hand's lawyer, William Colby, with the details of Colby's upcoming trip to the Far East. Inside his briefcase were the names of prominent Australian politicians and business personalities with dollar amounts handwritten in the five and six figures (*Mother Jones*, August/September 1987).

The circumstances behind how Hand met

Frank Nugan, a local lawyer and heir to a food-processing fortune, have never been properly clarified. Under oath, at the inquest, Hand claimed he couldn't remember.

The bank grew and had offices or affiliates in 13 countries. According to Jonathan Kwitny, whose book *Dope, Dirty Money, and the CIA: Crimes of Patriots* (1987) documented the scandal, the bank did little banking. However, over its seven-year existence it amassed large sums moving, collecting, and disbursing money. As soon as investigators began looking into the affairs of the bank in 1980, it was declared insolvent. Kwitny discovered that in the immediate days after his death, Nugan's house was taken over by Hand, Yates and Houghton, as company files were packed in "cartons, sorted, or fed to a shredder" (*Mother Jones*, August/September 1987). Its branch in Chiang Mai, Thailand, writes Kwitny, was the most mysterious of all of Nugan Hand's activities. Why was a supposedly legitimate bank opening an office in Chiang Mai, a region awash in the opium-growing trade?

After much investigative work, Kwitny discovered that the Chiang Mai branch of the Nugan Hand Bank was on the same floor in what he believed to be the same suite as the United States Drug Enforcement Agency office. When asked, the DEA wouldn't offer an explanation. Kwitny found that every which way he turned he was stonewalled.

He finally hit pay dirt when he tracked down Neil Evans, an Australian who was selected by Hand to run the Thailand branch. Evans reported to Kwitny that during his seven-month stint, Hand told him to deposit $2.6 million from six major drug dealers. Another employee at the Bangkok office said, "There was nothing there but drug money." (Before releasing it to the public, the Joint Task Force on Drug Trafficking, an investigation commissioned by the Australian government, deleted ten pages on Nugan Hand's Thailand activities from its report.)

The bank collapsed, owing some $50 million. None of the deposits were secured because they were used for illegal activities. These included defrauding American military personnel in Saudi Arabia out of nearly $10 million. The bank sent out "investment counselors" to installations where Americans were working in Saudi Arabia and told them to invest their salaries in Nugan Hand's Hong Kong branch in secured government bonds.

The Australian government eventually investigated the collapse of the bank and found that millions of dollars were missing and unaccounted for. It discovered that the main depositors of the bank were connected with the narcotics trade in the Middle East and Asia, and that the CIA was using Nugan Hand to finance a variety of covert operations. Government investigations revealed ties between Nugan Hand and the world's largest heroin syndicates. The reports said that the Bank was linked to at least 26 separate individuals or groups known to be associated with drug trafficking."

In 1983 the Australian Joint Task Force on Drug Trafficking released a report on Nugan Hand's activities to Parliament which said Shackley, Secord, Clines, Quintero, and Wilson were people whose background "is relevant to a proper understanding of the activities of the Nugan Hand group and the peopl associated with that group."

The investigations also detailed Nugan Hand's involvement in the sale of an electronic spy ship to Iran and arms shipments to South African-backed forces in Angola which were being supported by the CIA. These operations were run by Edwin Wilson, a career CIA officer who in 1983 began serving a 52-year prison sentence for selling tons of weapons and training expertise to Libya. Wilson claims he was set up to cheat him out of his fair share of the profits of the Secret Team's covert operations.

Confirming Nugan Hand's illicit activities and spilling a few beans of his own, in 1983 Wilson's business partner, Frank Terpil, told journalist Jim Hougan:

"The significance of Miami is the drug syndicate. That's the base. Shackley, Clines, the Villaverde brothers, Chi Chi, Rodriquez¾all the people that I hired to terminate other people, from the Agency¾are there. Who's the boss of Clines? Shackley. Where do they come from? Laos. Where did the money come from? Nugan Hand. The whole goddamned thing has been moved down there. . . . Clines was running drugs . . . The pilot of the plane in Asia was Dick Secord, a captain in the Air Force. . . . What was on the plane? Gold! Ten million bucks at a time, in gold. He was going to the Golden Triangle to pay off warlords. The drug loans. . . . Now what do you do with all the opium? You reinvest it in your own operation. Billions of dollars — not millions — billions of dollars" (*Covert Action*, Information Bulletin, Summer 1987).

None of those involved in the scandal have ever been convicted of any crimes as all eventually fled Australia.

Marchetti says that Nugan Hand is a good example of a unique type of covert operation: an independent group of people with ties to the CIA are in business for themselves, but at the same time carry out tasks for the CIA. The group is in a position to do the agency special favors, such as laundering money or providing cover for secret operations. The agency, in turn, will use its influence to throw business the company's way or t offer the company protection from criminal investigation" (*Mother Jones*, August/September 1987).

In light of the scandal, Kwitny concludes that "the license to commit crimes in the name of national security has been granted too often and too lightly." He asks some very relevant questions the American people should also ponder: When agents of the U.S. steal, when they get involved in drug deals, how far should the patriotic cloak granted by national policy stretch to cover them? Does it cover an agent who lines his pockets in side deals while working in the name of national security? (*Mother Jones*, August/September 1987).

Iran

After the fall of Saigon in April 1975, the focus of operations for the Secret Team moved to the Middle East. Shackley was now in Washington as CIA Associate Deputy Director in the Directorate of Operations. Clines was in Washington as head of CIA operations training. Richard Secord was appointed chief of the U.S. Air Force's

Military Assistance Advisory Group, which represented U.S. defense contractors selling arms to the Shah's army and training them in the use of this new military equipment. The secret team was also advising the Shah on how to use sophisticated communications equipment so his secret police force, SAVAK, could contain the regime's adversaries and political opponents.

One major military contract the group maintained during this time was Rockwell Intrnational IBEX's electronic and photographic surveillance project for intelligence gathering, not only in Iran but in the entire region, including the then-Soviet Union. On August 28th, 1976, three of the top managers of the project were shot dead while driving through Teheran. Officials blamed Libyan-trained Islamic Marxist guerrillas (*Washington Post*, August 29th, 30th, 1976), but Gene Wheaton, a longtime U.S. military investigator and former IBEX Director of Security, says that these people were killed to cover up a scam which skimmed profits from the IBEX project.

From the start, IBEX was plagued with corruption. According to a report in the *Washington Post*, a month before the assassinations, U.S. ambassador to Iran Richard Helms and a former CIA head, sent a handwritten letter to then-CIA Director George Bush complaining about the project and urging him to investigate allegations of corruption (*The Nation*, August 27th, 1988).

Wheaton discovered that Secord, Clines, Quintero, and Albert Hakim had a "historical record of skimming off of military projects, taking kickbacks" and that they had laundered large amounts of payoffs for military programs in the Middle East through Swiss bank accounts. Gene Wheaton testified in a deposition for the Christic Institute that the three Rockwell men "were murdered to cover misdeeds on the project, a project where Albert Hakim served as the bag man and that this was part of the Ed Wilson network." He claims that John Harper, who served as head of security for the project from November 1976 to May 1977, was told by Frank Terpil after the murders that the "Rockwell matter" had been taken care of.

Afghanistan

In May 1980 Dr. David Musto, a Yale University psychiatrist and White House advisor on drugs, discovered that the CIA and other intelligence agencies denied the White House Strategy Council on Drug Abuse he was heading access to all classified information on drugs. He warned then that what happened in Laos would occur in Afghanistan. Another White House Drug Council

Member, Dr. Joyce Lowinson, writing the *New York Times*, accurately questioned: "Are we erring in befriending these tribes (Afghanistan and Pakistan rebel tribesmen) as we did in Laos when Air America helped transport crude opium from certain tribal areas?"

They were both right. After President Carter began shipping arms to the mujahideen guerrillas in December 1979, drug-related deaths in New York City rose by 77 percent *(The Progressive,* July 1991). By 1982, Southern Asia, although never before a source, supplied 60 percent of the U.S. heroin market.

University of Wisconsin professor Alfred McCoy says that during the more than ten years of CIA covert support for the mujahideen resistance, the Bush-Reagan Administration and the mainstream media said almost nothing about the involvement of leading Afghan guerrillas and Pakistan military in the heroin traffic.

McCoy tracks the relationship between the CIA and the narcotics trade in Afghanistan and Pakistan to a May 1979 meeting at Peshawar in Pakistan's Northwest Frontier province between a CIA envoy and Afghan resistance leaders chosen by Pakistan's ISI (Inter Service Intelligence). The ISI was said to offer an alliance with its own Afghan client, Gulbuddin Hekmatyar, leader of the small Hezbi-i Islamic group, rather than a broad spectrum of resistance leaders (*The Progressive*, July 1991).

It's never been fully explained why, but when eagan and Bush took office Pakistan-U.S. relations soared. More than $3 billion in U.S. aid, including F-16 fighter jets, flowed to General Zia's army. In return, Zia allowed the CIA to open an electronic intelligence station in northern Pakistan aimed at the Soviet Union. This enabled U.S. spy flights over the Indian Ocean from Pakistani air bases near the Persian Gulf.

With CIA and Pakistani support, Hekmatyar became Afghanistan's leading drug trafficker. In May 1990, the *Washington Post* published a series of articles explaining how the United States had ignored Afghan complaints of heroin trafficking by Hekmatyar. The newspaper reported that Hekmatyar commanders close to the ISI ran laboratories in southwest Pakistan and that ISI cooperated in its heroin operations.

McCoy says that during the time the mujahideen were being supported by the CIA, their opium harvest doubled to 575 tons. Once these mujahideen elements brought the opium across the border, they sold it to Pakistani heroin refineries operating under the Pakistani government's protection (*The Progressive*, July 1991).

In September 1985 the Pakistani newspaper

The Herald reported: "The drug is carried in National Logistics Cell [part of the Pakistani Army] trucks, which come sealed from the Northwest Frontier and are never checked by the police."

Drug Enforcement Agency officials admitted that the shipment of CIA weapons into Pakistan played a key role in allowing the trade in heroin to flourish. No heroin was refined in Pakistan before 1979 but now Pakistan produces and exports "more heroin than the rest of the world combined," one agent told the *Philadelphia Inquirer* (February 28th, 1988).

The free flow of heroin had a devastating effect on the Pakistani people. Addiction rose to 5000 in 1980, to 70,000 in 1983, and to more than 1.3 million by 1985. At more than $10 million in sales made each year from the sale of heroin, it was larger than Pakistan's governmental budget and equal to more than one quarter of the gross national product.

When investigative journalist Larry Lifschultz began looking into the ties between General Zia and the Afghan drug trade, he discovered that European and Interpol police investigations of the major heroin traffickers had been aborted at the highest levels of the Pakistani government. The U.S. Drug Enforcement Agency itself had 17 agents working out of the U.S. Embassy in

Islamabad and compiled reports on 40 narcotics dealers in Pakistan. Yet not a single major syndicate was investigated by Pakistani police.

Typical of the misinformation that had blocked U.S. action against Pakistan's heroin trade, the State Department's semi-annual narcotics review in September 1988 called General Zia "a strong supporter of anti-narcotics activities in Pakistan."

"Once the CIA has invested its prestige in one of these opium warlords, it cannot afford to comprise a major covert action with an investigation," McCoy points out. "Respecting the national security imperatives of CIA operations, the DEA keeps its distance from agency assets, even when they are the major drug lords" (*The Progressive*, July 1991).

Nicaragua

The Secret Team's activities can be connected from Cuba, to Laos, through Iran, and to Nicaragua. It was the same network, the same people, and the same set of covert operators. The reasons the CIA became entangled with drug traffic in Central America were the same as they were in Burma and Laos.

Victor Marchetti contends that the CIA got involved with the Kuomintang drug runners in

Burma because they, too, were resisting the drift towards communism there. The same thing happened in Southeast Asia, and in the 1980s in Latin America.

"Some of the very people who are the best sources of information, who are capable of accomplishing important tasks to stifle communist movements, happen to inhabit the criminal world," he says. "The CIA keeps getting involved with these kinds of people, not for 'drug purposes' or for personal gain, although that has become a major part of it, but to achieve the higher ideological goal of fighting communism" (*Frontline*, May 1989).

The use of drug profits to finance the Contra war was confirmed in April 1989 by the Senate Foreign Relations Subcommittee on Narcotics and Terrorism. Chaired by Senator John Kerry of Massachusetts, the investigation discovered that, through a web of business relationships with Latin American drug cartels, the Contras were supplied with "cash, weapons, planes, pilots, and air supply services." The subcommittee found that senior officials in the Reagan-Bush White House were fully aware that the Contras were shipping drugs into the United States, but did nothing to stop it.

"The logic of having drug money pay for the pressing needs of the Contras appealed to a number of people who became involved in the covert war," the report of the Subcommittee stated. "Indeed, senior U.S. policy makers were not immune to the idea that drug money was a perfect solution to the Contras' funding problems."

Daniel Sheehan says that evidence of drug trafficking by the Contras and their supporters centers on three related allegations: that a major "guns-for-drugs" operation existed between North, Central, and South America and that helped finance the Contra war; that the Contra leadership received direct funding from major drug dealers; and that some of the Contra leaders themselves have been directly involved in drug trafficking.

Some of these allegations come from less than ideal sources. For instance, Pilot George Morales says after he was indicted in the spring of 1984 for drug trafficking that he was approached by Contra leaders offering him "a deal." If he set up a Contra drug-smuggling operation, his indictment would be "taken care of by people in Vice President Bush's office." He agreed, and flew weapons to John Hull's ranch (a liaison to the Contras) and returned with narcotics (CBS's *West 57th St.*, April 6th, 1987). Morales said his planes landed at Hull's ranch in Costa Rica.

Gary Betzner, one of Morales' pilots, said he himself took two tons of small-aircraft weapons and returned to Florida with a thousand kilos of cocaine (*Out of Control*). In March 1986 another pilot, Michael Tolliver, flew 28,000 pounds of weapons to Honduras and returned to South Florida with 25,360 pounds of marijuana (*Newsday*, April 6th, 1987). "I smuggled my share of illegal substances, but I also smuggled my share of weapons to the Contras in exchange, with the full knowledge and assistance of the DEA Drug Enforcement Agency and the CIA," Betzner claims (*Newsweek*, January 26th, 1987).

The cocaine originated from Pablo Escobar and Jorge Ochoa, Colombian drug traffickers who worked with the Medellín cocaine cartel. The drugs were shipped to John Hull's ranch and then sent on to the U.S. Two Cuban Americans, Felipe Vidal and René Corvo, arranged the money transfers. Hull, Vidal, Ochoa, Escobar, and Corvo were defendants in the Christic Institute's lawsuit.

Ramón Milián Rodríguez, chief accountant of the Colombian Medellín cocaine cartel, who is currently serving a 43-year prison sentence for money laundering, told CBS News and the Senate Foreign Relations Subcommittee that he personally arranged to have $10 million of Colombian drug money funneled to the Contras from late 1982 through 1985. "The cartel figured it was buying a little friendship," Milián Rodríguez told congressional investigators. "What the hell is 10 million bucks? They thought they were going to buy some goodwill and take a little heat off them" (*Newsday*, June 28th, 1987).

When Congress cut of funding for the Contras in 1984, replacement funds had to be found. Milián Rodriguez testified that although he had been laundering foreign payments for the CIA up through 1982, the CIA turned to him again (*Frontline*). He says he used Cuban-controlled front companies in Miami to funnel the money to the Contras, and that the money pipeline to the Contras was arranged by CIA veteran Felix Rodriguez, who would call him and tell him where to drop the money (*Out of Control*).

"To have people like me in place, that can be used, is marvelous for them," Milián Rodríguez points out. "The agency, and quite rightly so, has things that they have to do which they can never admit to an oversight committee, and the only way they can fund these things is through drug money or through illicit money that they can get their hands on in some way (*Frontline*). Adds General Paul Gorman, the commander of the U.S. Southern Command in Panama from 1982 to 1985: "If one wants to organize an armed resistance or an armed undertaking for any purpose, the best place to get the money, the easy place to get the guns are in the drug world."

Probably the most disturbing aspect of the entire connection of drugs to the Bush-Reagan White House's Contra supply effort is the way Congress dealt with the issue. For instance, on July 23rd, 1987, Senate and House Select Committee investigator for the Iran-Contra Affair Robert Bermingham sent a memo to Co-Chairman Senator Daniel Inouye and Congressman Lee Hamilton, requesting them to issue a statement stating that the investigative staff found no direct evidence of Contra involvement in drug trafficking. Yet Bermingham hadn't even consulted with the investigator on the Senate Foreign Relations Committee looking into the Contra-drug link (*Boston Globe*, July 29th, 1987).

To their credit, some politicians, like Senator John Kerry, did try to investigate the matter. He learned that not everyone was as earnest as he was in getting at the truth. He discovered that Richard Messick, a Republican staff member of the committee, was believed to be passing documents and information to the Justice Department (*Village Voice*, July 14th, 1987). Messick was also found to be relaying misinformation from the Justice Department to discredit witnesses before the committee.

The Christic Institute was the only investigation that got even as far as the courts. Yet its lawsuit was eventually dismissed by a Miami judge¾as Sheehan believes, because of intervention by the Justice Department in the judicial process.

Prior to this decision David Corn wrote an article in *The Nation* (July 2nd, 1988) entitled "Is There Really a 'Secret Team'?" which put the entire affair into perspective. Corn was critical of the effort by the Christic Institute. He thought Sheehan was trying to do too much: to make a legal point, as well as to educate the American people of the evils of the national security apparatus in order to rally public opposition to it. "These various aims," he writes, "though, can collide with one another. The reliance of a Secret Team may work fine given the confines of a RICO suit. Outside, however, it may undermine the Christic Institute's broader public education campaign, which aims to raise questions about the national security state and U.S. foreign policy as a whole."

Corn argues that by ascribing the events in the affidavits as the work of a "Secret Team," it lets the CIA, the Pentagon, the State Department, and various Administrations off the hook. For instance, the secret war in Laos was a massive, and official, CIA operation with the support of a full range of U.S. government agencies. It wasn't carried out exclusively by a "secret team" of covert operators.

Edith Holleman, a Christic Institute lawyer,

says that these actions should be considered non-governmental because those involved were acting above and beyond their authority, even if they were employed by the U.S. government. She believes journalists are making the mistake of not seeing the cas as a legal finding. "Lawsuits," she adds, "are not history books. They're only parts of history books. To suggest that these events reflected a pattern of government action is to look at it from a political scientist or historical perspective. Are the courtrooms the place to decide the crucial issues of political analyses?"

Corn wondered whether the individuals in the Secret Team were (are) acting on behalf of themselves, or the "enterprise"¾the term which the Christic Institute eventually began using after it was brought out in the Iran-Contra hearings¾or were semi-official agents of the CIA.

"With its advocacy of the Secret Team theory," Corn writes, "the Christic Institute has painted itself into a corner. If all these ventures are the handiwork of a few rogues, there is no reason to worry about the national security system at large. What's the remedy for a few bad apples? Better screening of personnel. . . . If anything like the Secret Team exists, the issue is the system that spawned it." Corn believes that the guilty party is not the Secret Team, but rather decisions made by Presidents and Vice Presidents, in most cases, supported by the entire national security bureaucracy, to employ the Secret Team (*The Nation*, January 27th, 1992). The question is whether the system that spawned it can stamp it out?

A more important question is whether George Bush knew that his office, through his National Security Advisor, Donald Gregg, was associated with and jointly carried out operations together with elements of Latin America's drug cartel? If so, what does that say about the Reagan-Bush Administration's so-called "war against drugs"?

Snookering Saddam: the Hidden Agenda in the Persian Gulf War

After supporting Saddam Hussein secretly for nearly eight years, why did the White House so eagerly want to go to war with him? In fact, only two years previously, Under Secretary of State Robert Kimmitt stated his belief at a 1989 meeting of the National Security Council that Iraq was "influential in the peace process" and "a key to maintaining stability in the region." (*Wall Street Journal*, December 7th, 1990)

The most common reason given by administration officials (after the fact) was that the Saudis, America's long-standing vested interest in the region, were petrified of the Iranians winning the Gulf War and thus consuming the Persian Gulf with Islamic Fundamentalism. Yet this assertion was never confronted.

Iran-Contra player Richard Secord told me personally that this explanation held little water: "The pro-Iraqi tilt came fairly early on in the Reagan administration. I was against it. I don't know of any responsible opinions, militarily speaking, who believed an Iranian victory would cause a Muslim fundamentalist tide to sweep over the rest of the Arab world in a domino-like fashion."

Nor does the argument that the U.S. supported Saddam to strengthen bi-lateral trade between the two nations make much sense either. After the Iran-Iraq war, Iraq was heavily in debt. The Administration had to lend Saddam the money to buy American food, equipment and weapons, and violate U.S. law to have the Atlanta branch of the Italian bank BNL provide Iraq with loans for its missile program.

Another line the apologists used was that "if the U.S. had better relations with Iraq it would reform Saddam's record on human rights." President Bush said on one occasion that the U.S. tried to help Iraq to "bring Iraq into 'the family of nations'."

These arguments should regarded as highly suspect. Morality rarely defines relations between foreign leaders, national interests do. (If this statement came from Jimmy Carter it could be mores readily accepted. For some reason former CIA director George Bush is just not easily associated with motivations like human rights concerns and morality.)

If the the White House's main consideration in supporting Saddam was to reform his evil ways, why didn't every other ruthless dictator in the world receive loan guarantees to purchase food and advanced military technologies? There is absolutely no indication that either the Bush or Reagan administration cared one iota about Saddam's human rights records. In fact, it was Congress who had to urge the White House to enact sanctions against Iraq after the gassing of the Kurds in 1988.

Nor should the claim that the Administration "failed to understand the true nature or intent of Saddam's regime" or that the "intelligence community failed to inform the White House of the Iraqi build-up," be readily believed. Statements such as these completely disregard the wealth of information available to modern statesmen. Former President Bush knew the exact nature of Hussein's regime as well as he knew that of other Middle East dictators such as Hafez Assad of Syria. It simply makes no sense that every newspaper columnist, rabbi, political analyst, and analyst at a think-tank can understand that guys like Hussein and Assad are nasty people, but the President of the United States, armed with all the intelligence and high quality information available to his vast staff, remains in the dark, naive, and duped by one of the most blatant dictators of our era. (Doesn't the Oval Office subscribe to *Time*, *Newsweek*, *The New Republic*, *Commentary*, and *The American Spectator*?)

Arguments that the White House policy went "astray" and "took on a life of there own" are equally ridiculous. The direction of foreign policy can change in a matter of days. Sanctions can be imposed almost immediately. If the Administration discovered that Saddam had gassed the Kurds or was building a nuclear bomb, and didn't like it, they could have stopped their support for Saddam in seconds.

A more logical reason why the Reagan and Bush White Houses may have gone to such lengths to arm and support Iraq may have been the hostility Bush and other members of both administrations had towards Israel, which promoted the Level Battlefield Doctrine (LBD) the Administration used in balancing its Middle East policy.

This doctrine, which was never publicly acknowledged by the White House, is based on the notion that the problem in the Middle East is not with the Arabs, but in Israel's reckless use of its military superiority. Therefore the Administration must ensure that the Arabs are put on a parity with Israel militarily so that Israel will be pressured into concessions. This, it was believed, would in the long term satisfy the Arabs.

This explains why as soon as Bush became President in 1989 support for Iraq intensified. Bush must have wanted to teach Israel a lesson for all the times the pro-Israel lobby in the U.S. killed another arms deal with the Arabs. When Bush got into the Oval Office, he could finally get even.

This, ofcourse, does not account for Bush's war against Saddam, which may have been due to a completely separate secret agenda, remaining to this day hidden from Congress and the American people. This was the need to have U.S. troops stationed in Saudi Arabia to man the $200 billion string of military bases there called CENTCOM. These bases were considered vital by the White House for strategic control of the world. They were too valuable to be left in the hands of the Saudis.

A war was needed to see whether the $200 billion investment in CENTCOM, a combination of communication and air defence systems, infrastructure, and weaponry, was justified.

In addition to containing 60% of the world's known oil reserves, the Persian Gulf is in the soft underbelly of the Soviet Union. It completes a circle of U.S. influence in the Middle East: Egypt, Turkey, Pakistan, and Morocco. The only way to get to Africa from the Soviet Union is through Egypt or Saudi Arabia.

CENTCOM was considered to be crucial to American interests in the region. Former National Security Adviser Frank Carlucci claims: "We created in the Pentagon, CENTCOM, a separate command for the Middle East to serve America's vital military purposes in the region."

CENTCOM was also an integral part of the covert U.S.-Saudi relationship and one of the best kept secrets of the Reagan and Bush Administrations.

Some Reagan administration officials, like former Defence Secretary Casper Weinberger, told me that the reason for the AWACs sale was strictly "to give greater defence capacity to Saudi Arabia". Others, like Geoffrey Kemp, who was a member of the National Security Council, concede that "The Saudi Arabian bases were a part of the overall game plan."

The most sophisticated part of the CENTCOM system is its Command, Control, Communications, and Intelligence capabilities. It is much more than the ability of computers to network information. It is the ability to create an accurate picture of all data available at any moment. Although it is probably the most advanced system of its type in the world, it's worthless without the software, or the operators.

Scott Armstrong, a former reporter for the *Washington Post*, an investigator for the Senate Watergate Committee, and co-author with Bob Woodward of *The Bretheren*, followed this covert relationship since the AWACs debate in the early days of Reagan's first Administration.

Armstrong says that, along with CENTCOM, the series of bases the Americans have built in Saudi Arabia were crucial to Desert Storm. Had they not been there, it might have taken a year or two to defeat Iraq. Had the CENTCOM network not been in place, he doubts the Administration would have pushed for war.

"Bush wanted to breathe life into the bases," he says. "Without them we wouldn't have known what targets were hit, or what the enemy was up to. More SCUDS would have hit Saudi Arabia and Israel. The system is the reason why the Iraqi air-force didn't get off the ground. Radar, missiles and planes would have operated with less than one-quarter of their efficiency and accuracy. Decisions could be taken in hours which would have taken weeks or even months in other battlefields. Would we still have won? Yes, but not without losing 30,000 or 40,000 lives."

Armstrong points out that there is no written treaty between Saudi Arabia and the United States. Congress knows only that the U.S. has a strategic relationship with the Saudis, but they don't know the details of it.

"Although no defence pact exists, the U.S. does have an "unwritten", but explicit obligation to defend the Saudi royal family. Both sides realize that if the two countries exchanged a piece of paper with a signature on it, it would be considered a treaty and would have to be presented to Congress, which might not ratify it." AWACS, he points out, passed by only two votes in a Congress controlled by the Republicans. "Would Congress accept America's commitments to NATO if they were simply the result of a series of discreet decisions? This is exactly the relationship the U.S. has to the Saudis."

It was the AWACS debate, which Armstrong covered for *The Washington Post*, that first started his investigation into America's secret relationship with the Saudis. He says that the figures that were being given to Congress about the scope of the sale were slanted. While the Administration claimed the value of the military equipment being sold to Saudi Arabia was $550 million, it was at least ten times that much.

Also, more than 90% of the value of the deal was left unaccounted for. The AWACs deal provided a cover for the construction of the bases as only about $50 million of the entire $5.5 billion package was for the AWACs planes. Armstrong says that he was told by Richard Secord, then Deputy Assistant Secretary of Defence for the Middle East, that 90% of the arms package were for "spares, training and ground equipment."

"Nobody asked how could it be that the planes only made up 10% of the value of the contracts," says Armstrong.

With the American public focused on the AWAC planes, the rest of the deal snuck through. To keep the debate out of the public eye, the Saudis agreed to an American plan for a simple oral understanding between the then head of the Saudi air force, Colonel Fahd Abdullah, and the chief of the U.S. military group in Saudi Arabia, Major General Charles L. Donnelly Jr. (*Mother Jones*, November/December 1991)

Armstrong maintains that the key issue in this "secret agenda" was to minimize congressional review by breaking down military purchases into smaller packages that were below the dollar limits requiring congressional approval. One method used was instead of purchasing military aircraft, having Saudi-acquired commercial jets upgraded to military specification with avionics obtained from other countries.

Little press or congressional attention was paid to these deals because the Administration used private corporate think tanks, such as Boeing Corp, BDM Corp and Mitre Corp, to advise the

Saudis on how to construct the overall system. Mitre told the Saudis to integrate their radar, missile systems, fighters, and command-communication posts into one network, similar to the NORAD system in the U.S. or NATO's NADGE. The country was divided into five regions with each having its own system and operating center, linked together into a central headquarters by satellite.

Armstrong says that each was capable of commanding an air war from Egypt to Pakistan, or from the southern Soviet Union to the Indian Ocean.

When he checked on the Saudi side, Armstrong found that the AWACs sale was part of a deal that involved sending the U.S. Rapid Deployment Force to the region in the event of war. The Saudis agreed that they would pre-position essential material for the Rapid Deployment Force to use. Through all this, Armstrong discovered that the series of superbases and weapons systems for use by the U.S. in event of a war were all "off the books".

Little was heard about the secret bases after the AWACs sales were approved. A few years later Pentagon sources told him that information on the matter had been compartmentalized and that members of the cabinet, the NSC, and even the President didn't really know all the details. Oliver North would later tell him it was part of a "loose arrangement" between the U.S. and Saudi Arabia.

The major question now is what type of access will the U.S. have to these network of bases and weapons systems in the future? The Saudis want to minimize the U.S. presence on their soil while at the same time they realize there has to be enough of a U.S. military presence to serve as a viable deterrent.

"The U.S. wants to preposition equipment there but the Saudis say no, we will man the bases," says Armstrong. "The U.S. says we can't rely on non-U.S. servicemen to operate the equipment. I believe Secretary of Defence Dick Chaney promised the Saudis that the secret relationship could continue in secret, and that no admission of a permanent U.S. base would be made nor any public treaty."

Camouflaged in a secret clause of the 1981 deal to sell AWACs to Saudi Arabia, it was the CENTCOM program that Israel most feared in the AWACs sale, not the AWACs themselves.

The Plot to Sucker Hussein into Invading Kuwait

Needing a war in the region, how did Bush then go about getting one? By suckering Hussein into it.

It remains a mystery why in late July the Kuwaitis weren't trembling with fear as 500 Iraqi tanks and 100,000 troops were poised on their border. Instead of trying to appease Saddam, they mustered the courage to stand up to him, even thumbing their noses at him. Yet literally minutes after the first cannon shot was fired, the Kuwaiti royal family were on planes bound for their short life in exile. Could Bush have tricked Hussein into believing that the U.S. would sit back and do nothing if Kuwait was invaded?

In the best tradition of his mentor, General Henry Stimson, Bush believed that it was time for America to go to war to boost national pride and to rid the country of the Viet Nam complex complex for good. The scandal over the collapse of the nation's Savings and Loans was in the headlines. Neil Bush was in trouble. For President Bush, there was no better time for a war.

Nor is it too difficult to believe that Saddam would think that with all the support and aid he had received from the U.S., the last thing for the Americans to do would be to wage war on him. All Bush had to do was lead Hussein to believe that the U.S. wouldn't interfere if he invaded Kuwait.

What about a secret deal between the U.S. and Saudi Arabia? We may never know because Bush refused to explain what he was referring to when he informed Congress on August 9th, 1990 that he received "requests" from King Fahd and Kuwait. Months later, when asked repeatedly, the Administration would still not reveal either to the House or the Senate the nature of these "requests" or the U.S. response to them. This refusal violated the Case-Zablocki Act of 1972 which obliges the Secretary of State to submit to Congress within 60 days the substance of all international accords, written or oral. (*Time*, Nov. 19th, 1990)

Secret cooperation between the Kuwaitis and the CIA certainly existed before August 1990. A document released to the *Reuters* news agency after the Iraqi invasion of Kuwait, revealed that Brigadier General Fahd Ahmad-al-Fahd, the chief of the Emir's security forces, visited the CIA from November 12 to 18, 1989 and met with CIA chief William Webster. Part of the agreement was the training of 128 of the Emir's personal bodyguards, as well as offering of American help in computerizing the Kuwaiti State Security Department. The CIA admitted that Webster met al-Fahd, but called the document a forgery. (*Village Voice*, March 5th, 1991)

Another secret agreement may have led directly to Hussein's invasion. A summit was held in Jedda, Saudi Arabia on July 31st, 1990, between Hussein, Saudi King Fahd and the Emir of Kuwait. Kuwait pledged $10 billion to Iraq to help pay its war debts.

In May 1990 at a Gulf Cooperation Council meeting, Saddam had demanded $30 billion. The Kuwaitis eventually reneged on the $10 billion offer and told Saddam they would only contribute $500,000. Thus it's possible that Hussein might have moved his troops up to the Kuwaiti border as a means of pressuring Kuwait into coughing-up more money. (*Village Voice*, March 5th, 1991)

Jordan's King Hussein intervened in the negotiations and tried to convince the Kuwaiti royal family to be more conciliatory toward Iraq, urging them not to underestimate the Iraqis. However Sheikh Sabeh told him, "We are not going to respond to Iraq...if they don't like it, let them occupy our territory...we are going to bring in the Americans." (*Village Voice*, March 5th, 1991)

A few days later King Hussein claims the Emir told his senior military officers that if the Iraqis invade, they must hold them off for 24 hours. He is reported to have told them "American and foreign forces would land in Kuwait and expel them." In a note to Saudi King Fahd, the Emir of Kuwait said: "We are stronger than they (the Iraqis) think."

From Arms to Avocados: The Mysterious World of Amiram Nir

No book on the covert relationship between Israel and the U.S. would be complete without a chapter on Amiram Nir, who has in his time served as both the counter-terrorism advisor to former Israeli Prime Minister Shimon Peres and as the pointman for Oliver North in the Iran-Contra deals. Because of his untimely death in a mysterious plane crash on December 1st, 1988 in Mexico, the world may never find out the whole story behind Irangate. Yet Nir, perhaps more than any other player in the scandal, knew things that would have embarrassed, if not put behind bars, numerous American and Israeli leaders.

At the time of his death Nir was said to be in Mexico on "unspecified business". It was also rumored that he was involved in a plot to corner the world's avocado market, had sold arms to the Mexican government, and faked his own death.

Four months later, in March 1989, West German arms merchant Herman Moll added to the mystery when he told the German-based *Middle East Insider* that the CIA sabotaged the aircraft because Nir "knew too much." Moll explained that Nir was privy to details of the South American drug cartel's involvement with White House efforts to resupply the Contras. He further claimed that Nir had extensive knowledge of how $15 million in profits from arms-sales to Iran had disappeared from secret bank accounts in Switzerland and wound up in Contra hands.

At the age of 34, Amiram Nir was put into the newly created post of Advisor on Counter-terrorism to Prime Minister Peres when the Labor party leader took over the Israeli government in late 1984. He had previously served as party spokesperson, campaign manager in Peres' failed 1977 bid for the premiership, and then later as a military reporter for Israeli Television.

Although he had achieved the rank of lieutenant colonel in the Israel Defence Forces, had gone through an intelligence course, and commanded an armored corps in the reserves, the Mossad balked at his political appointment claiming he was not qualified for the post of Counterterrorism Advisor. Perhaps he wasn't, but it's believed that Peres needed someone from outside the traditional ranks of the Israeli intelligence community to coordinate future arms sales to Iran, and Nir fit that bill.

When the story broke of secret dealings between the U.S. and Iran in the Lebanese journal, *Al Shiraa* in November 1986, North wanted Nir to take the blame for the diversion scheme, but Nir refused. After resigning from government service in March 1987, Nir apparently opened a London-based regional sales office for an unidentified Israeli security firm. Friends of his said he was also involved in both arms and oil contracts in Mexico.

One story, (which I believe was deliberately planted to create a cover for Nir) was published in *Newsweek* in August 1989 and contended that Nir was involved with a company called Nucal de Mexico, which purchased an avocado-packing plant in Uruapan, in the Mexican state of Michoacan.

Local exporters in Uruapan became riled when they discovered that Nucal was shipping between 16 and 20 tons a week and controlling more than a third of the export market. They claimed Nucal was part of a scheme cooked up by the Israeli government, which already controls 80 per cent of the European avocado market, to corner the world avocado market by selling at a temporary loss to European importers.

A Nucal employee, Carlos Mendez Vega, admits to "escorting" Nir around while he was on "avocado business" and the head of Nucal, Israeli-born Avraham Cohen, told the weekly that Nir had interviewed him for that job, implying that Nir was his boss or part owner in the firm.

Nir arrived in Mexico City from Madrid on November 28th and immediately flew to Uruapan with an unidentified Italian partner. According to the Michoacan state attorney general's office, when Nir chartered the two-engine T210 Cessna from the Aerotaxis de Uruapan commuter airline, he identified himself as "Pat Weber" (Nir's codename in the Iran-Contra affair Nir was Mr. Miller). Federal Judicial Police commander in Uruapan Jose Luis said Nir used his own name at the hotel he stayed in.

The police report revealed there were two other passengers in the aircraft. The pilot, Guillermo Guahonte, and a 25 year old mysterious Canadian woman, Adriana Stanton, survived. A fourth passenger, Pedro Espionoza Hurtado, whose circumstances for being on the plane were never ascertained, died instantaneously.

Stanton registered for the flight under the name "Ester Arriaga" but an inspector at the departure wing at the airport declared that both Nir and Stanton used their real names. A few days after the crash David Goan, whose father is Nissim

Goan, a Swiss-based Jewish millionaire and one of the owners of Nucal, confirmed that Stanton worked for his company in the quality control department. Nir, he said, did not. He would not confirm whether Nir owned a share of the firm nor what his relation, if any, he had to it.

When asked at her hospital room about her connection to Nir, Stanton told *The Associated Press* "it was a coincidence, we shared the same plane." On an unscheduled flight?

Isauro Gutierrez Fernandez, a spokesman for the Michoacan state Attorney General's office said that Stanton was serving as Nir's "guide." Juan Manuel Ortea, an inspector at the Uruapan airport, told police Stanton was employed as Nir's "secretary."

Pedro Cruchet, an Argentine citizen living in Uruapan illegally and employed by Nucal, initially identified and recovered Nir's body for the police although he couldn't explain how he happened to be near the crash site. When asked to prove his own identity, he claimed he'd lost his ID at a bullfight. Nir's body was then whisked back to Israel and quickly buried without an autopsy.

When a young woman answered the door to a *Washington Post* reporter at Stanton's hospital room she indicated that Cruchet was present. When she went to get him another woman appeared at the door and told the journalist that

Cruchet wasn't there and that she had never heard of him. The second woman reiterated that Stanton's presence on Nir's rented Cesna had been "purely a coincidence" and that Ms. Stanton had no connection with "the Israeli". She refused to identify herself other than to say she was in Mexico as a tourist from Argentina.

John Picton, a feature reporter for *The Toronto Star* who investigated the plane crash was told by U.S. intelligence sources that they had information leading them to believe that Nir wasn't dead and had undergone a face-lift in Geneva- "where the clinics are very good, very private and very discreet" and would be able to disguise his identity. When Picton told that to Stanton's mother in her Toronto home she replied:' "That's strange. It's the second time we've heard that." She wouldn't reveal the other source to Picton nor would her daughter speak to Picton or confirm whether she did or did not work for Nucal or Nir.

Considering the mystery surrounding his presence in Mexico and the aliases he and Stanton used, perhaps avocados were not the only commodity Nir was peddling. When asked by the Hebrew daily *Yediot Aharonot* in the spring of 1987 if after leaving government he might enter the arms business, he replied: "I've had enough of missiles." Had he? "I'm going into other types of business," he declared. Did he?

A week after the crash the Long Island-based daily *Newsday* reported that U.S. intelligence sources in Mexico believed Nir to be the middleman for a large arms deal of Israeli weapons passing via a port in Vera Cruz on the eastern coast of Mexico. It quoted American drug enforcement agency officials as saying that there had been a steep rise in the efforts of cocaine smugglers to transport drugs from Michoacan to the U.S. and that three weeks prior to Nir's visit a captain in the Mexican army confirmed that a "large shipment" of Israeli made weapons arrived at the Vera Cruz port and was transported to Mexico City. The sale was made, according to the captain, by a group of Israeli arms dealers, not the Israeli government.

If Nir was killed in Mexico, before he got on the plane, as most investigators of the incident seem to believe, it is likely he was silenced for what he knew about soon to be inaugurated President George Bush. When Bob Woodward of *The Washington Post* interviewed Nir in London six months before he was killed, Nir said he was considering the best way to tell his side of the story, as "only half of the Iran-Contra affair had been made public." Regarding the failed mission to Teheran in May 1986, "more than half of this trip is not known." Nir then asked him not to publish any parts of the interview until he got the go-ahead. When Woodward contacted Nir again in early October he was told that he was still not ready to go public.

Other than perhaps Shimon Peres, Nir knew more than any other Israeli about the quantity and types of arms which were sent to Iran, how much was paid, where the money went, and who profited from the sales. The Israeli government confiscated all of his notes and papers, which were never to be made public, and contained records of Nir's discussions and meetings with American and Iranian officials. The Israeli government also forbade him from answering questions to the U.S. Justice Department and congressional committees. In fact, despite his key role, he is the only player in the Iran-Contra affair who never publicly testified, or even commented on his role to the press.

His silence may have been due more to self-interest than selfless discretion. Nir remained in government after the rotation of the Prime Ministership from Shimon Peres to Yitzhak Shamir in October 1986. In March 1987, after telling his new boss that he was taking a vacation in London, he instead flew to Geneva. There, at the luxury Reserve Hotel, he met with Ghorbanifar. The Saudi billionaire Adnan Khashoggi, who provided the financing in earlier arms sales to Iran, was also registered at the hotel.

That same week, by coincidence, Albert Hakim, a close business associate of General Secord who would eventually be found guilty of the misdemeanor of "supplementing" North's government salary, was also in Geneva. It is believed that Ghorbanifar held accounts at the Credit Suisse bank, the bank Khashoggi used to finance two or more U.S. arms sales to Iran, and also the bank North, Hakim and Secord used to process Iran arms sales profits.

One month later Israeli intelligence sources discovered that an official of the Credit Suisse bank resigned after his contacts with Kashoggi and Ghorbanifar were revealed. Did these bank records show that someone in the Israeli government acted as a conduit to pass part or all of the $3.5 million in profits to the Contras? Did Nir personally profit from the deals (as it is widely believed that Secord and Hakim did)? Were they making another deal?

Those same bank records in Switzerland could have become a nightmare for certain Israeli government officials, namely Prime Minister Peres. They would shed light on why the Israeli government never allowed Nir (or Schwimmer and Nimrodi) to testify before Congressional investigations. Was Peres worried that Nir would disclose that it was his role in the diversion of money from the Iranian arms sales to the Contras or that he personally authorized the establishment of the fund to initiate covert anti-terrorist operations?

Indeed, Nir knew a great deal about U.S. and Israeli arms sales to Iran because he was the intersection everyone's activities passed through. He must have known who set up the Swiss accounts, who controlled them, and how much went to the Contras and how much to middlemen like Ghorbanifar and Secord. He sat in on crucial meetings in Teheran, Frankfurt, Washington, Tel Aviv and London. He knew about all the covert operations and where the money originated from to fund them.

In an interview with *Yediot Aharonot* after leaving office in March 1987, Nir said that Shamir went out of his way to protect Nir's name and reputation, in Israel and in the U.S.. Peres, on the other hand, simply "left him to the dogs." He added, "the moment you need support from him, (Peres) vanishes."

This remark, in context as part of the one public statement he ever made about Iran-Contra, says a mouthful.

Dov Yudkovsky, then editor-in-chief of *Yediot Aharonot* as well as Nir's father-in-law, pressured Peres to give Nir a position in the government. Nir had worked hard on Peres' election campaign in 1984 and felt he deserved the position of cabinet secretary. When that spot was given to Yossi

Beilin, Yudkovsky kept asking Peres to find something else for Nir to do.

From November 1984 to December 1985 Nir spent his time trying to build contacts in the intelligence field. As an outsider, this wasn't an easy task, but, according to a close aide of Peres, Nimrod Novik, Nir was creative and dynamic. He sought out areas that others weren't interested in. Peres had him contacting businessmen and diplomats to pick up any information he could.

The combination of being a former journalist and a political appointee appalled Mossad officials. When they found out that he was using these back channels they feared he would jeopardize their agents and intelligence assets. According to key government sources, it was then Defence Minister Yitzhak Rabin who was the most hostile to Nir, even getting into shouting matches with Peres over his work.

Although Nir wasn't part of the usual Israeli intelligence network, he became privy to documents which explained all the sensitive details of the American-Israeli covert relationship since the early 1980s. Knowledge of these operations may have led directly to his death.

While many investigators of Nir's mysterious death have surmised that the CIA was behind Nir's death, so far only one man familiar with CIA activities has broken his silence. He is Lieutenant Navy Commander Robert J. Hunt. In June 1993 Hunt began providing information to investigator/author Rodney Stich, author of the books *Defrauding America* and *Unfriendly Skies* about CIA scandals and cover-ups during the 1980s. Hunt gave Stich ample documentation on his secret work for the CIA, and of his work for The Mossad. In a letter published in Stich's book dated October 4th, 1993, the Consulate General of Israel in Chicago, Yaacov Nir (no relation), confirmed that Hunt was involved in the now famous May 1986 secret trip to Teheran which included Amiram Nir. Hunt was also involved in Operation Cappuccino, which sent TOW missiles from the U.S. to Iran to secure the release of American hostage Ben Weir.

Hunt claims the CIA killed Nir in Mexico. He says he first met him at the King David Hotel in Jerusalem on July 29th, 1986 while guarding then Vice-President George Bush at the meeting mentioned in the section on Bush's Iran Contra involvement. Nir briefed Bush about the ongoing sale of U.S. arms via Israel to Iran. Hunt discovered later that Nir was secretly taping the entire conversation. Hunt says Nir was killed when Bush found out that Nir had recorded the conversation and thus had evidence linking Bush to the arms for hostage deal.

At that meeting, Nir outlined for Bush efforts

taken throughout the past year "to gain release of the hostages, and that a decision still had to be made whether the arms desired by the Iranians would be delivered in separate shipments or for each hostage as they are released."

Hunt says that also in attendance at the meeting were two assets of the CIA, Charles McKee and Matthew Gannon, both subsequently killed on board Pan Am Flight 103, which was blown up over Scotland. A number of investigative journalists have claimed that McKee and Gannon were the primary targets of the Pan Am bombing.) Hunt says that Bush discovered that Nir had secretly tape recorded the meeting and was planning to expose the activities involving Bush and arms sale to Iran, which also would have exposed many high level U.S. officials. The decision was then taken to kill Nir.

At CIA headquarters in Langley, Virginia, Hunt had met Oliver North and asked him what had happened to Nir. North told him that Nir was killed "because he threatened to go public with the recording of the Jerusalem meeting in 1986."

According to a book published by SPI Books in early 1994, *Compromised: Clinton, Bush and the CIA*, former CIA operative Terry Reed presents compelling proof that Nir had extensive knowledge of the Reagan administration's ties to drug traffickers in Central America and of the use of drug profits to finance the Contra war in Nicaragua. Reed had met Nir a number of times in Mexico on various missions and had exchanged information with him. He says that as the Contra war was conducted through Vice-President Bush's office, Bush and his aide Donald Gregg would have had to have had knowledge of drug profits being used to purchase weapons for the Contras.

The use of drug profits to finance the contra war was confirmed in April 1989 by the Senate Foreign Relations Subcommittee on Narcotics and Terrorism. Chaired by Senator John Kerry of Massachusetts, the investigation discovered that through a web of business relationships with Latin American drug cartels, the Contras were supplied with "cash, weapons, planes, pilots, and air supply services." The subcommittee found that senior officials in the Reagan-Bush White House were fully aware that the Contras were shipping drugs into the U.S., but did nothing to stop it.

"The logic of having drug money pay for the pressing needs of the Contras appealed to a number of people who became involved in the covert war," the report of the Subcommittee stated. "Indeed, senior U.S. policy makers were not immune to the idea that drug money was a perfect solution to the Contras' funding problems."

Evidence of drug trafficking by the Contras and their supporters centered on three related allegations: that a major "guns-for-drugs" operation existed between North, Central and South America to help finance the contra war; that the Contra leadership received direct funding from major drug dealers, and that some of the Contra leaders themselves have been directly involved in drug trafficking.

Pilot George Morales says that after he was indicted in the spring of 1984 for drug trafficking, he was approached by contra leaders offering him "a deal." If he set up a contra drug-smuggling operation, his indictment would be "taken care of by people in Vice President Bush's office." He agreed and flew weapons to John Hull's ranch (a liaison to the Contras), and returned with narcotics. (CBS West 57th St., April 6th,1987)

Morales said that his planes landed at Hull's ranch in Costa Rica.

Gary Betzner, one of Morales's pilots, said that he himself took two tons of small aircraft weapons and returned to Florida with a thousand kilos of cocaine. In March 1986 another pilot, Michael Tolliver, flew 28,000 pounds of weapons to Honduras and returned to South Florida with 25,360 pounds of marijuana. (*Newsday*, April 6,1987)

"I smuggled my share of illegal substances, but I also smuggled my share of weapons to the Contras in exchange, with the full knowledge and assistance of the DEA Drug Enforcement Agency and the CIA," Betzner claims." (*Newsweek*, January 26th, 1987)

The cocaine originated from Pablo Escobar and Jorge Ochoa, Colombian drug traffickers who worked with the Medellin cocaine cartel. The drugs were shipped to John Hull's ranch, then sent on to the United States. Ramon Milian Rodriguez, chief accountant of the Colombian Medellin cocaine cartel, currently serving a 43 year prison sentence for money laundering, told CBS News and the Senate Foreign Relations Subcommittee that he personally arranged to have $10 million of Colombian drug money funneled to the Contras from late 1982 through 1985.

"The cartel figured it was buying a little friendship," Milian told congressional investigators. "What the hell is 10 million bucks? They thought they were going to buy some good will and take a little heat off them." (*Newsday*, June 28th, 1987)

When Congress cut off funding for the Contras in 1984, replacement funds had to be found. Rodriguez testified that although he had been laundering foreign payments for the CIA up through 1982, the CIA now turned to him again. He says he used Cuban controlled front companies in Miami to funnel the money to the Contras, and that the money pipeline to the Contras was arranged by CIA veteran Felix Rodriguez who would call him and tell him where to drop the money.

"To have people like me in place that can be used, is marvelous for them," Rodriguez points out. "The agency, and quite rightly so, has things that they have to do which they can never admit to an oversight committee, all right, and the only way they can fund these things is through drug money or through illicit money that they can get their hands on in some way."

General Paul Gorman, the commander of the U.S. southern command in Panama from 1982 to 1985, adds: "If one wants to organize an armed resistance or an armed undertaking for any purpose, the best place to get the money, the easy place to get the guns are in the drug world."

If Nir was threatening to implicate Bush in operations which linked the White House in million dollar business ties with drug traffickers, it is little wonder that the CIA (i.e. Bush) came to the conclusion that Nir had to be eliminated.

Even after Nir was killed, however, there was still damning evidence that had to be destroyed.

Nir's tapes and diaries about U.S. government involvement with drug traffickers were the target of the mysterious burglars who broke into the Tel Aviv suburb home of Judy Nir Moses, Nir's widow, in late July 1991. The family claims they knew who sent the burglars to break into the house and that tens of recordings and documents were taken which contained information "that would attack certain people."

The police said that the thieves did a "clean job" and that nothing else was disturbed and that the thieves knew exactly what they were looking for. There was no sign of a break-in and they took no valuables.

The burglary came at an unusual time, during an Israeli police investigation into whether top Israeli officials and middlemen were involved in the disappearance of millions of dollars paid by the Iranians for weapons. Also taken were exact details of the financial dealings in all aspects of the Iran Contra affair that Israel was involved in.

Indeed, Nir had enemies in Israel who may have wanted his personal papers and diaries destroyed for good. One of them was Yaacov Nimrodi.

Nimrodi, an Iraqi-born Jew who spent many years in Teheran advising and training the Shah's secret police, became a conduit for the Israeli arms industry to Iran. When Khomeini came to power in the late 1970's, he returned to Israel. As part of the Irangate deals, Nimrodi was involved in two shipments of missiles in July and August of 1985. Nimrodi has always claimed that he never made any money from the arms sales, but arranged them for "humanitarian reasons", to help secure the release of Americans held hostage by Shiite groups controlled by Iran.

In June 1991 an Israeli police investigation was opened to determine if Nimrodi withheld profits from the sales from the Defence Ministry.

A month later Nimrodi made a public declaration in a Tel Aviv court stating that he had acted on his own behalf in his arms dealings with the Iranians and thus all the profits from the deals were his. He claimed he earned $37 million from the Iranians, but after paying for the missiles and other expenses, says he took a loss on the deal of nearly $750,000. (*Inside Israel*, August, 1993)

The police closed their investigation of Nimrodi without any of the details being made public. Then, in March of 1993, Yitzhak Tubiahu, an Israeli businessman living in London, filed papers in a London court contending that he and Nimrodi had been equal partners in an arms business since 1983 and that Nimrodi owed him $1.7 million from the Irangate sales. Nimrodi doesn't deny he was once a business partner of Tubiahu, but insists Tubiahu was not involved in the Irangate deals.

After examining the documents of arms sales with Nimrodi, Tubiahu claimed that $3.5 million were earned from these transactions, and thus Nimrodi owed him $1.75 million. With interest, the sum amounted to $4 million.

Tubiahu tried to verify the list of expenses Nimrodi had claimed he incurred, many of which however were "anonymous payments in cash." When Tubiahu did track down some of the people who Nimrodi listed as receiving money for various types of services, they all denied being involved in the affair or even knowing Nimrodi.

Nimrodi claims that Tubiahu sent a letter to senior government officials threatening that if he didn't receive his fair share of the Irangate deals, he would tell all he knew about bribes paid to "certain politicians."

Nir's papers and recordings may have been stolen for another reason. It is known that from April 1990 through June 1992 until he left office, Prime Minister Shamir's Office had been gathering files and documentation on Bush's involvement in Iran Contra. During the entire Presidential campaign of 1992 it seemed that not a week went by without some reference being made to the Bush administration arming Saddam Hussein or Bush knowing about the Iranian arms-for-hostages deal in the U.S. press. Those leaks were coming from Israeli sources in an effort to put pressure on Bush. Nir's death at the hands of the CIA, just weeks before Bush took office, was probably what kicked that covert slug-fest off in the first place. American-Israel relations have never been the same since.

Terrorism Against
The United States

Hot New Titles of Jewish
Interest from S.P.I.